The Four Secrets *of* Retention

Other Books
by Fran Dramis

The CIO Handbook:
How to Avoid Having CIO Mean "Career Is Over"

Creating an Intentional Business Life:
How to Direct your Career Path to Provide Fulfillment

The Four Secrets of Retention

Holding Mindshare in a Transitional World

Francis "Fran" Dramis

Alpharetta, GA
ISBN: 978-1-61005-873-5

Library of Congress Control Number: 2016921275

10 9 8 7 6 5 4 3 2   0 1 1 2 1 7

Printed in the United States of America

♾This paper meets the requirements of ANSI/NISO Z39.48-1992 (Permanence of Paper)

I would like to dedicate this book to my family and to those people who have been so supportive of me over the course of my forty years in business. The support of my family was my foundation for being able to accomplish what I set out for in my career. And the support of those who worked with me and alongside me proved to be the real secret of my success in achieving my life goal.

Contents

Preface   ix
Acknowledgments   xiii
Introduction   xv

Chapter 1
The Last Gold Watch   1

Chapter 2
The Challenge for IT Leaders   19

Chapter 3
What Matters Most   45

Chapter 4
From Job Security to Life Security   65

Chapter 5
The Real Secret of Retention—Business Life Goals   75

Chapter 6
Linking to Life Events   95

Chapter 7
Living My Business Life Goal   103

Endnotes   113
About the Author   117

Preface

What does retention really mean in today's business world? What does holding onto someone mean nowadays, now that the average tenure of an employee is only five years—one-third to one-fourth what it was before the downsizing decade of the 1980s?[1]

If you are an experienced leader, you may already know that it is a difficult and often losing proposition to get people to stay and work with you for an extended period of time, especially among the people in your staff— those with the experience and responsibility that enables you to achieve your goals.

Today, retention is really more a matter of *attention*, of capturing the mindshare of your leaders for the brief time that they are with you. This is the definition of retention that I use throughout my book, for I believe this orientation is critical when you consider the implications. For however loyal and engaged your leaders are for the five or so years that they are with you, so too are the one hundred or one thousand or ten thousand people in your organization who are being led by them.

Retaining loyalty and mindshare are real challenges for leaders *of* leaders today. A generation ago, there was the promise of a career with one company, and retention was measured in the number of years someone stayed on the job. Up until the 1980s, a "career" meant spending the better part of a lifetime working for one company, and after thirty years, receiving a gold watch and retirement party. There was loyalty, though, and the role of a leader was to mentor his or her direct and indirect reports up the corporate ladder. Unfortunately, that era has long since passed, along with the promise of job security.

In all of this, the concept of a "career" has changed. Today, it's up to the individual to define his or her own business path and to make the right choices to ensure personal growth and success. For many, especially those in the rapidly changing field of technology, that path has become a series of company moves in order to build out personal knowledge and experience. And for many, even among the best and brightest, that path is not always clear or as well planned out as it could be.

My intent is to show leaders that by improving the personal marketability of their senior staff, linking them to their company's strategic direction, enveloping them in a values-based organization, and becoming their **Business Life Mentor**, they will remain loyal to you and the company for the short time they are with you in the course of their business lives. In my experience, true retention only lasts as long as these four elements are present. Once they are gone, your people will move on as well.

My premise is not that these four principles will ensure that someone will spend his or her remaining working years—or a large part of them—with you. My proposition is that you as a leader will be able to retain the hearts and minds of the leaders in your organization, and you'll encourage the best out of each of them during the part of their business lives that they are with you.

I found great success with this orientation toward retention. For over thirty years, in the midst of significant technological change that accelerated the demand for strong leadership at all levels, I maintained a senior staff of over five hundred assistant vice presidents, directors, and supervisors, and over that period of time, I lost only one whom I did not want to lose.

Competing for the best and the brightest is a challenge when top organizations are offering young talent a great job with a powerful brand name and attractive perks. This book is a guide in how to do exactly that—how to compete for that talent.

My message in this book is a simple one: If you as a leader can connect with the aspirations of your employees and help them achieve their **Business Life Goals**, talented people will be loyal to you and your organizations for the time that they are with you and for as long as their work has them on the right path. Moreover, they'll be fully engaged and highly productive because they are building on their life security.

Acknowledgments

I wish to recognize John Fayad (www.theliterarycoach.com) for his invaluable help in the writing of this book.

Introduction

Over the course of my nearly forty years of business life, I have had the opportunity to lead and be a part of some amazing organizations and institutions. This occurred during the explosive decades of the 1990s and 2000s with transformational discoveries and inventions in science and technology. In that time, the entire context of commerce and communications changed.

That was the setting during my years with the Wall Street investment bank Salomon Brothers, bringing new capabilities to trading; as a transitional IT leader with Coopers & Lybrand, Citibank, NASDR, and Banker's Trust, tasked with transforming their technology organizations; and in my role as EVP, chief information officer, and eCommerce, and security officer for the BellSouth Corporation, where I refined my practice of "leader as mentor."

Those were challenging but exciting times as companies looked to their IT organizations to make the most of their respective technological revolutions. In reflecting on what made the IT organizations that I led so remarkable in their camaraderie, inventiveness, and productivity, I realize that I was able to connect with the valuable leaders in my organization and mentor them toward their **Business Life Goals**.

The Four Secrets of Retention shares how I was able to make that connection with my direct and indirect reports in a deeper and more valuable way. It is intended to inform leaders that the best way to keep and motivate employees is to provide them the skills and knowledge that will make them more marketable and put them on the path to achieving their **Business Life Goals**, even if their goals ultimately take them beyond the walls of your organization or company.

It may seem counterintuitive, but in doing this, leaders are able to tap into the psyche of the young, talented, and highly demanded individuals who in this new century do not have any expectations of a "career" with any one company, but rather expectations of themselves and their own business life path. That wasn't the thinking in the last century, but times have changed.

From Job Security to Life Security

The downsizing that occurred in the 1980s proved to many Americans that the concept of "job security" no longer existed. Story after story of companies shedding thousands of employees anchored the realization in the minds of every employee and college graduate that no job was "cradle to grave" any longer.

That extensive reduction in the workforce devastated Baby Boomers and affected the lives of many Gen Xers. Millennials, though, were the first generation to accept fully that there was no such thing as job security. That acknowledgement is clearly reflected in their job-turnover rates.

I believe the youngest of the Gen Xers and most all Millennials today accept the work world for what it is and generally don't have a sense of company loyalty. Nor are companies showing employees any loyalty through career-path training—a subject that I define more fully in Chapter Two.

I faced each of these challenges as an IT leader for the two decades following the downsizing of the 1980s. Yet by reorienting the mindset of my first- and second-line reports from the hope of "job security" to the certainty of "life security," I was able to retain highly talented and, in many instances, critically valuable technologists in spite of the intense competition for their services.

I believe that by creating a **Business Life Plan** with direct and indirect reports, and providing employees the skills and knowledge they need to achieve their **Business Life Goals**, a leader can be virtually assured of retention and the highest levels of productivity.

When their **Business Life Plans** are developed, employees will have established a series of three-year **Business Life Segments** needed to reach their **Business Life Goals**. And most importantly, it is in that intersection of the skills obtained from the job segment they're engaged in and the skills needed to progress toward their **Business Life Goals** that leaders create the most engaged, most loyal, and most productive employees.

This mentoring process that I'm proposing in my book enables leaders to inspire people to stay and not just work, but work at their very best. The focus is entirely on the individual and making him or her more marketable. All the other motivating factors such as salary, signing bonus, choice of geographic locations, free cafeteria, daycare, dry cleaning, and all the other amenities can easily be matched by any company competing for talent. I believe talented people are looking for something more.

Helping an individual define his or her **Business Life Goal** and the plan to achieve that goal will create a "stickiness" with the employee and gain the most productivity out of an individual than any benefit or perk a leader can offer.

I followed this leader-as-mentor path instinctively throughout my time on Wall Street and in a more formal, practiced way at BellSouth. At BellSouth, every one of my direct reports and all their direct reports knew of their **Business Life Goals** and had a **Business Life Plan**. Every one of them was engaged in a relevant **Business Life Segment** and highly motivated at it. That is precisely how and why they won all those awards!

And the competition then with the likes of Microsoft, IBM, Oracle, SAP, and any of the other huge bell-operating companies was as fierce as it is today with Apple, Facebook, Google, Twitter, and other big-brand, high-tech companies.

This is a guidebook for anyone who wishes to be a leader or who is currently a leader in any type of organization, whether it's a business, a sports team, a community association, or a church group.

There have been many great books written on the best practices of top-performing companies, and it's retention of talent and engagement that often tops their lists of areas of focus. These books do a great job in defining *what* it takes to create high-performing organizations. There are few, though, particularly in the field of technology, that delineate exactly *how* to connect with individuals in order to make those best practices come to life. And making that connection is more difficult now given the short time employees stay with any one company.

The Bureau of Labor and Statistics today measures job tenure every two years, and as of January 2016, the median number of years that employees had been with their current employer was 4.2 years, down from 4.6 years in January 2014. When you break it down by age in 2016, the tenure of workers ages 25 to 34 years (2.8 years) is less than three times that of workers 55 to 64 (10.1 years).

Retention of management has been steadily declining since 2010 and is now at 5.1 years, down from 5.7 years in 2014.[2] Further up the ranks, CIOs at large enterprises stay with their companies for an average of 5.7 years.[3]

The point in all this is that the promise and expectation of a career with one company has changed dramatically over the past forty years. I believe this means that the concept of retention and what a leader can hope for in holding onto an employee has to change as well.

This is not a book about *what to do*, but rather a book about *how to do it*. And the two technology organizations that best exemplify the "how to" in connecting with individuals are spotlighted in this book: Salomon Brothers and BellSouth.

As managing director and CIO of Salomon Brothers, the company's IT organization shifted from being a back-office, secondary-focused organization to one of the most valued IT groups on Wall Street. We produced some of the most innovative products ever offered from the financial center of the United States.

During my tenure at BellSouth, their IT organization went from the bottom half of the top one thousand to the top 25 percent, right through to winning *CIO* magazine's Enterprise Value Award in 2005. Over the course of my years at BellSouth, the IT and security groups were repeatedly recognized as top organizations in their fields and received numerous national awards to show for it:

- *Computerworld*'s 100 Best Places to Work in IT (2000, 2002, 2003, 2004, 2005)

- Top 10 in Diversity category—*Computerworld*'s 100 Best Places to Work in IT (2004)

- SecurE-Biz Leadership Award, 2005

- *CIO* magazine's Enterprise Value Award, 2005

- *InformationWeek* 500 Most Innovative Users of Technology (Ranked #10 in 2005)

During my tenure, I was also named one of the country's top IT leaders and recognized by a variety of publications:

- *CIO* magazine's CIO 100 Award, 1999
- *CIO* magazine's Top 100 Leaders for the Next Millennium, 2000
- *Computerworld's* Premier 100 IT Leaders, 2002
- CIO Lifetime Achievement Award, 2016

The Four Secrets of Retention is designed to be a concise desktop guide for leaders that quickly gets to the crux of "mentor-leadership," and through my business life experiences, provides leaders a template for how to facilitate the process of helping employees determine their **Business Life Goals** and develop the **Business Life Plans** and **Business Life Segments** that ultimately lead to those goals.

While the first four chapters define the business environment leaders are struggling in today, trying to retain and motivate employees, chapters five through seven are instructional, showing leaders exactly what to do to build loyalty and retain their key people.

I believe the role of a leader today is to unearth their direct and indirect reports' **Business Life Goals** and make it tangible and visible for them. In Chapter Five, I provide a mentoring process to help leaders help individuals think through what would have them feel fulfilled at the end of their business life and how to programmatically chart a path comprised of **Business Life Segments** that makes that end point of fulfillment tangible and possible.

This chapter will contain examples and stories of employees who grappled with the task of defining their last day at work and **End-of-Business-Life Paragraph** by not using terms that describe their position, but rather what they are actually doing on their last day that characterizes their **Business Life Goals**.

Chapter Six focuses on the process that a leader must go through in order to be a part of an employee's **Business Life Goal**. It describes how a leader must align with each individual through the development of a **Business Life Plan** and the **Business Life Segments** that comprise that plan.

This chapter also shares the implications and consequences of entering into this mentoring process with the individual, and the various outcomes that it creates, including mentoring people toward developing realistic **Business Life Goals**, and in Chapter Seven, mentoring in more personal areas of family and life.

A Simple Message to Leaders

My intent in writing this book is to pass on to the next generation of leaders the mentorship and guidance that they would have received from me had they been my direct and indirect reports. My wish is that they will read this and experience the same personal growth and success.

This book is a guide in how to do exactly that: how to compete for that talent, how to retain individuals by making them more marketable, and how to put them on the path to success and the attainment of their **Business Life Goals**.

My message to leaders in this book is a simple one: if you can connect with the aspirations of the people you are leading and help them achieve their **Business Life Goals**, talented people will remain loyal to you and their organizations and they will not leave. Moreover, they'll be fully engaged and highly productive because they will be building on their life security through you.

Chapter 1

The Last Gold Watch

It was the late 1990s and I was attending a retirement party for my then father-in-law. He had joined Exxon-Mobil in the 1960s and, after having worked there thirty years, was receiving his gold watch, promised to him on his first day of employment and presented to him now for having remained loyal to the company for all those years.

As the ceremony got underway with my father-in-law's family alongside and his closest peers and notable supervisors from the company in attendance, I couldn't help but think about the events in my own business life as a young technologist and technology leader. The past thirty years had ushered in a complete transformation of the American business environment, and I thought to myself, *I'm watching the last episode of a passing era.*

What made the moment even more poignant was that Exxon-Mobil—actually, the oil and gas industry itself—was, in essence, the last bastion of the gold watch. It stood to reason. It was one of the last industries that had not yet experienced the ravages of downsizing in the '80s and '90s. The oil and gas industry was not known for innovation and change, and the product itself, taking millions of years to produce, had little to no competition.

Thirty years of memories filled my mind that day. As I watched and listened, I recalled how my business life had started, how corporate life in America, in less than a generation, had changed forever, and how as a leader in those turbulent times I found a way to replace that gold watch for my employees with something more meaningful and of far greater value.

A Very Different World

Many people believe that life in the 1950s and 1960s was a simpler and more satisfying time. Some say that it was the best time in America. There was an upbeat, anything-is-possible mood in the country following World War II. America began to prosper, and by 1950, the strength of the nation's economy had, in one way or another, positively touched every American's life and the outlook of many American workers. Job security, how much workers earned, and the cost of goods were all directly related to the health of the nation and its economy; and during the 1950s, the American economy was the strongest in the world.

Much of Europe and Japan were in post-wartime recovery, and there was generally no foreign competition for our hard goods such as automobiles, appliances, and steel. We were the manufacturing kings—the only game internationally. This gave American corporations enormous control over the marketplace, in the pricing of products, and even in the pace of new product introductions. American business was set on cruise control, and the horizon was all blue sky as far as the mind could imagine.

A social contract, or "job-security pledge," was typically offered to the generation of Americans following World War II—a cradle-to-grave job with steady progression up the corporate ladder for those who wanted it and put in the hours to earn it. In the '50s and '60s, companies took care of their employees, and it was not uncommon for people—like my father-in-law—to work for one company for decades.

Employees were loyal to their companies and dedicated to their jobs, and many stayed with the same organization for their entire career. After thirty or forty years, there would be that long-awaited retirement party with a plaque and gold watch engraved with their name alongside the company's logo.

The same security pledge existed for Baby Boomers and Gen Xers joining the workforce in the '70s and early '80s. Job security was expected; it was part of the social fabric; it was the way life was. When you joined a company in the '70s, you expected that arrangement.

That was the expectation in my mind when I joined AT&T. I committed myself to working my way up as far as I could into the telecommunications giant and retire with my pension, my gold watch, and a great career experience. Even though I was a double major in history and education coming out of college, and my initial dream was to be a secondary education teacher and coach, I was swept up in the elation of belonging to a large and very successful company and the ambition of climbing their corporate ladder all the way to the top.

Sign Me Up!

I remember my very first job interview with AT&T and how I was pleasantly struck by the immediate and acknowledging response the VP of human resources gave to my one and only question: "What is the fastest way to becoming chairman of the board?"

I thought she was going to laugh herself out of her chair, but instead she replied, "We have an intense focus on technology today. We need people in programming, and we're training people right now to be programmers. The fastest way to climb the ladder, Fran—faster than anyone else—is to become a technologist."

She went on to explain that technology people were becoming very important to AT&T because technology was going to help the company control its costs. She said that if I joined the company as a technologist, I would be able to skip over management levels. She explained that the pay grades for technologists were more than the traditional wages being paid out at comparable grades, and that the technology jobs were nonunion jobs. She went on to explain that they weren't management jobs either, but that they did pay at a management scale. So my "above-pay-grade" salary would enable me to jump over management levels.

I was sold and immediately said, "Sign me up!"

She responded, "That's fine, however, you first need to be trained in programming and be a member of this upcoming programming class." I straightaway signed up.

There were twelve people in my training class, and on the first day we discovered something that we apparently didn't pick up during the recruitment pitch. If any of us didn't score at or above 85 out of 100 on our weekly test, we would lose our job; not just the current position there at AT&T, but lose our job with the company. It dawned on me that they were dead serious. The pressure to succeed in that classroom every day and every week for eight months was very real and intimidating—and I loved every minute of it.

Of the initial twelve, eight of us made it through. I finished at the top of the class and went on to pursue my career in technology at AT&T, advancing quickly though the company's technology ranks and, simultaneously, management ranks. I regarded my goal of wanting to become the CEO or chairman as a process of moving through the company's seven levels of management, and that's what I set my sights on—the seventh level. It traditionally took twenty-five years to get to the third level, but I set a new record and did it in nine.

Insecurity about future employment never crossed my mind—not with AT&T. From the depression of the 1930s through the 1980s, the telecommunications behemoth had never laid off a person and never downsized. "Ma Bell" was proud of that fact. It stood as a testament to the company's job-security pledge and promise to every one of its employees.

Automobile Industry
and Planned Obsolescence

From the 1950s through the 1970s, the US market became saturated with cars produced by the "big three" automakers: General Motors, Ford, and Chrysler. There was little to no new innovation, aside from those mandated as a result of government safety regulations.

General Motors, under the leadership of Alfred P. Sloan Jr., transformed the auto industry in the 1920s and 1930s through the concept of planned obsolescence. GM began to place most all of its R&D on largely superficial annual model and style changes, and Ford and Chrysler followed suit.[4]

The goal was to make consumers dissatisfied enough with their current car, which still most likely had years of useful life left in it, to trade in and hopefully up to a more expensive model. Sloan believed that it was only necessary that GM's cars be "equal in design to the best of our competitors . . . it was not necessary to lead in design or to run the risk of untried experiments."[5]

GM became the auto industry's leader in image and marketing, spending huge sums on advertising and devoting a great deal of attention to styling. The strategy of having different-priced lines of automobiles was used to exploit consumers' social and material aspirations to their fullest.

James Flink, an auto-industry historian, defined the GM strategy as "blanketing the market with a car at the top of every price range and encouraging the consumer to trade up from Chevrolet to Cadillac via Pontiac, Oldsmobile, or Buick."[6]

With that mindset, engineering was considered of lesser importance to style and cost cutting, and for the decades to follow from the 1960s through the 1980s, the automotive industry—as well as other industries—was building hard goods, from cars to electronics to appliances, to be changed out every three or so years with the effect of compromising the quality and innovativeness of products built in the United States.[7]

A Lost Opportunity

The industrial expert W. Edwards Deming presented an opportunity to US automakers in the 1950s to produce high-quality automobiles—but the auto executives didn't appreciate Deming's harsh rebuke and in many ways didn't comprehend Deming's approach. Deming placed blame for the automakers' failings and lower qualities of production on management and their practice of planned obsolescence. He lacked charisma and often delivered his message in blunt language, making little effort to charm and win over boards, CEOs, and executive committees. The *New York Times* described him as "a tall, formal man who habitually wore frayed three-piece suits and spoke to senior executives as if they were school boys."[8]

Deming criticized the method of quality control used by US manufacturers across a variety of industries in the 1940s and '50s. Under the quality-control system in the US, products were inspected for defects *after* they were made. In contrast, Deming maintained it was better to design the manufacturing process to ensure that quality products were created from the start.[9]

The Japanese didn't mind Deming's abruptness. In 1950, Japanese businessmen turned to him to help them rebuild their economy that was devastated in World War II. He taught Japan's manufacturers how to produce top-quality products economically, and the Japanese eventually used that knowledge to beat the US automotive and electronic industries at their own game.

It All Changed in the '80s

By the 1980s, the US was faced with foreign competition, the extent of which we never experienced before. Competition trickled then flooded in from Asia and Europe, and it soon dawned on us that we weren't quite as inventive and competitive as we thought. That realization came quickly to other industries as well, and we began downsizing our workforces to compensate for the losses in sales and market share.

In the decades that followed, Japan's automobile and electronics companies carved out huge pieces of the US and global marketplace for themselves. By the 1980s, the US auto industry had already lost a sizeable part of the

American car market to Asian auto companies, not to mention European automobiles from the UK, Germany, France, and Italy. The US electronics industry pretty much vanished. Japanese companies such as Sony, Panasonic, and Sharp were considered the premium brands.[10]

We should have seen this coming. We weren't vigilant; we weren't challenged and hungry. The majority of industries affected by offshore competition, primarily from Asia, included the automotive, electronics, machine-tool, and steel industries. In contrast to countries such as Japan, South Korea, China, and India, US companies had significantly higher costs. For example, US automobile manufacturers had an approximate $1,000 cost disadvantage for their cars compared to similar classes of Japanese cars.[11]

Only a small percentage of this difference in cost was due to labor, yet workers were among the first to be cut despite the surplus of middle managers and engineers—another point of criticism by Deming of Detroit auto executives. Other US manufacturers faced similar challenges, from higher per-unit costs to greater overhead than their Japanese counterparts.[12]

It was a shock to the system and many of the largest companies began downsizing, quite a few of them for the first time in their histories, including General Motors, AT&T, Delta Airlines, Eastman Kodak, IBM, and Sears, Roebuck and Company.

A Revolution in Technology

Paralleling this transformation of the US business environment and loss of hundreds of thousands of jobs to foreign competition was the explosive rise of technology. Over the course of the 1970s and early 1980s, IBM created a revolution in technology with the System/360 line of central processing units, or CPUs, the brains of the computer where most calculations take place.

The iconic IBM System/360 ushered in a new era in computing, representing a significant departure from the past in the design and build of computers. It was the first time IBM had restructured the internal architecture of its computers since the early 1960s.[13] The result was more computer productivity at a lower cost than ever before. This was the beginning of a new generation of computers and a brand-new future in applications to business, science, and government.

The IBM System/360 allowed for faster computing and faster analysis than any previous computer system. It allowed for programmers to use the new programming language, COBOL, or common business-oriented language. COBOL was the first high-level programming language for business applications, many of which were unique to business and had the potential to replace human involvement in the manipulation of data.

The IBM 360 also enabled greater access to information sources that were previously inaccessible through a new desktop device called a CRT, or cathode-ray tube, similar to the picture tube used in televisions at the time.[14] Through the intersection of the IBM 360, COBOL, and the CRT, online computing and online access to information became pivotal elements in eliminating the layers of management that manually did what computer programs were now able to do in a fraction of the time with minimal human involvement and with no errors.

Reconciling No Longer a Manual Process

The target of downsizing at AT&T was middle management—jobs that would be replaced with technology. The concerns over cost structure and cost containment became paramount issues within AT&T. Many middle-management jobs in telecommunications at the time, such as sending billing statements to customers and reconciling dividend checks sent to investors, were replaced by programmable billing systems and reconciliation systems.

The first program I personally wrote in the late '70s while with AT&T was a reconciliation system for AT&T dividends paid to investors. When an investor would cash his or her dividend check, it would reconcile against my files, confirming the amount of the check sent by AT&T. A process that, in years past, was most likely performed manually by a floor full of employees was now a single, infallible, inexhaustible computer program.

Downsizing was at its most intense in the late 1980s and early 1990s. In the United States alone, 3.5 million people lost their jobs in the ten years following 1987. The losses centered on eliminating layers of middle managers, a move forced by increasing global competition and the growth of information technology.[15]

Not only did the flood of international and domestic competition create waves of downsizing, it also created a need for cost reduction, and the way that need was met was through technology. While corporations were ending their social contract with their employees, the work didn't go away. People had to be replaced by something that would get the job done. That something was technology.

The downsizing in the 1980s proved that there was no longer any such thing as job security. Story after story of companies laying off thousands of employees created an atmosphere in virtually every industry that no job was going to be "cradle to grave" any longer. That had a sobering effect on the American worker—on boomers initially, and then their children. There was no longer the hope of a career with one company.

The Changing Face of Telecommunications

The US government has always favored breaking up monopolies with competition and most likely favored the discipline that international competition was bringing to the automobile and electronics industries. So, it stands to reason that they took notice when domestic competition came to the telecommunications industry through a company called Microwave Communication Inc., or MCI.

MCI began its advancement into the telecommunications market in 1968, when founder William G. McGowan organized the MCI Communications Corporation in his effort to take on the monopolistic AT&T. For more than a decade, MCI fought AT&T in court until finally in 1980, it won an antitrust lawsuit.[16] In essence, MCI singlehandedly initiated and accelerated the divestiture of AT&T.

By the 1980s, AT&T was structured such that the majority of the profit in its bell systems was sourcing from AT&T long distance. MCI reasoned that the cost of providing long distance was very inexpensive compared to the cost of providing residential and small-business services. So, MCI erected two microwave cell towers and started charging less than half of what AT&T was charging its customers for long-distance service, thus cutting into the cost structure of AT&T.

AT&T's immediate reaction was to try to use legal and governmental means to block MCI from competing, but the US government was determined to bring competition to telecommunications and began the process of splitting up AT&T.[17]

AT&T was divided into the seven Bell holding companies; Western Electric was spun off to eventually become Lucent Technologies; Bell Laboratories became a standalone R&D (research and development) enterprise; and AT&T was essentially left with only long distance. The layoffs that devastated Detroit and the automobile industry now reverberated through the legacy AT&T and the seven Bell operating companies in the late '80s and early '90s.

The layoffs in telecommunications were massive and felt in cities across the US. This time, it wasn't because of international competitors, but rather domestic competitors that were leaner and able to use new technology to chip away at the corporate monoliths that were slow to adapt and change.

"My Job Is to Make You the Twelfth Largest"

In the mid-1980s, I was pulled from my position as vice president of technology at Bell Laboratories and made vice president of technology for AT&T Information Systems, the newly formed competitive branch of post-divestiture AT&T. Information Systems was formed to sell long-distance services along with business equipment and other business products and services. My first hurdle in managing was that I had to downsize an IT organization—the first and only time as a leader that I was ever asked to do that.

On my very first day as vice president of technology, I was called into the CFO's office and told that, because of cost issues, I had to reduce my second-tier-and-below management team by 30 percent, and that I had one month to complete that task. Thirty percent meant I had to let go of one of the three directors who reported to me and five of the fifteen division managers who were working for those directors. The downsizing of my organization included at least thirty of the ninety district managers, who in turn had to reduce their direct reports by 30 percent. In total, this downsizing would eliminate approximately one thousand AT&T employees, all within a month.

I recall my first speech to my newly inherited technology organization when I said, "My name is Fran Dramis, and I'm here as the new head of technology. You are the sixth-largest technology organization in the United States, and my first task in the next thirty days is to make you the twelfth largest."

The people who worked for me were some of the best in the world in telecommunications, information technology, computer science, and engineering. So while I was downsizing, competition was upsizing. I was, in essence, making available to my competition the talent that they needed.

Technology organizations from that point on had terrific growth. Their work product was the key to future competitiveness for not only AT&T, but for companies across many industries—from electronics to trading on Wall Street to healthcare. Technologists were in high demand, and other companies immediately hired the majority of the thousand people whom I had downsized. In fact, one of the directors that I let go of became a director of computing at MCI.

The New Definition of Retention

Letting go of those hundreds of technologists while at AT&T was the first time in my business life that I had to reduce the size of an organization. From that point on, and for the most part, while the rest of the country was downsizing, I was actively engaged in upsizing. Yet, I had to replace the loss of that social pledge and the end of job security with something different. I knew that the concept of retention would be completely different now, and my expectation and approach would have to change as well. I had to contend with the changing attitudes of the people who reported to me. I had to capture their attention and retain their mindshare.

What I replaced it with was the promise that my IT organizations were going to implement new technologies, and that anyone working for me was going to learn new skill sets and with those new skills, they would become more marketable.

To make my staff more marketable and attractive to outside companies seemed counterintuitive, but I discovered it to be the first step in retaining the mindshare of my most talented leaders. I realized that they would only be with me for a short period of time, but in that brief span of time that we were together, I would retain their loyalty, engagement, and productivity.

I believe the most critical job leaders have today — particularly leaders in technology — is to make every effort to retain the hearts and minds of your highly skilled people for the short time they are with you and your company. As I expressed at the onset of my book, the implications of their engagement, or lack thereof, are considerable. For however loyal and engaged your leaders are for the five or so years that they are with you, so too are the one hundred or one thousand or ten thousand people in your organization who are being guided and encouraged through their leadership.

That effort in the retention of mindshare, in my estimation, has four components. I introduced the first one in this chapter, which is to make the people in your organization more marketable. The rest of this book will reveal to you the next three, which includes giving them the feeling that the output of their work is strategic to the company, creating a set of shared values that allow people in an organization to bond to one another, and connecting what they are doing in your organization to their **Business Life Goals**.

Chapter 2

The Challenge for IT Leaders

Much in the same way storms form when weather systems collide, the downsizing that swept the country in the 1980s and, in the same decade, the rapid growth and expansion of technology, created quite a disturbance in the business environment. There was then and still exists now a constant churn of employees coming into and leaving organizations, searching for a better working environment, looking to make more money, and hoping to gain more knowledge and experience.

Some industries have it stormier than others. While the average employee's length of time with a company is 4.2 years, employees in the tech, financial services, hospitality, and healthcare industries spend much less time than that.[18]

There have been a slew of employee-engagement surveys and reports conducted over the years in an effort to understand why the turnover rate is so high. But I believe the loss of the job-security pledge that I spoke of in Chapter One is the underlying factor that has impacted every industry, and the unending demand for highly skilled employees is most likely why the technology industry has the highest turnover rates of all other industries.[19]

Interestingly, Google and Amazon have some of the lowest retention rates, with both companies averaging about one year in retaining their technologists, even though these companies offer very competitive salaries and great benefits—and they are often rated as the best places to work.[18]

As both a technologist and technology leader, I stood in the middle of that storm and experienced the demise of the one-company career; I directly participated in the rise of technology, and I gained a frontline perspective into why technologists are so mobile-minded when it comes to their professions. The whole of it presented me with a line of sight into how to hold onto the best, and how to draw out of them their very best.

Over the course of my business life, I have learned that there are four practices a leader needs to engage in, beyond the money and the perks, in order to retain highly skilled employees:

1. Increase employee's marketability by exposing them to the latest technologies.
2. Instill in employees the belief that their work is strategic to the organization.
3. Create a set of shared values that binds individuals together as one.
4. Connect what employees are doing in your organization to their **Business Life Goals**.

When applied together, these four practices are a powerful force in retaining the mindshare of employees. Yet the fourth element is what requires the leader's utmost attention, for it has the power to create the greatest "stickiness" between the technologist and the organization. If while someone is spending time with you they are actually gaining experiences critical for their meeting their life goals, they will be incredibly loyal and will not want to move on from your organization.

There's another element in this that adds to the challenge. Technology companies also have the youngest leaders, managers, and employees of any industry. Silicon Valley is a magnet for Millennials and younger Gen Xers, individuals born since the late 1970s — around the time the technological revolution started to take on wings. Technology itself has a special attraction to young people, who were raised with tech gadgets since childhood. Because of their experience, they have the most insights and ideas into reshaping and advancing the technology. This first wave of those young tech pioneers, now in their thirties and forties, is the central focus of this book and should be the central focus of IT leaders.

The Education Begins

After serving as vice president of technology for AT&T Information Systems, I became president and chief operating officer for Telic Corporation, a company that provided budgeting systems to the then seven regional Bell holding companies as well as other telecommunications systems providers.

I had no problem retaining technologists at Telic. Not only were they more marketable because of their leading-edge work product, but they were also considered by most everyone in the company as being strategic to the organization because their work *was* the company's product.

Systems such as budgeting, billing, logistics, and reconciliation were at the core of the cost efforts underway among the telecommunications companies. My job was to operationalize Telic's systems by transferring them to software. In less than two years, I was able to convert the company into a software business, offering us broader market reach, better economies of scale, and higher profit margins.

In 1988, I left Telic and telecommunications for Wall Street where the demand for technology was exploding. The need for investment firms to improve their capabilities and competitiveness in areas such as stock trading, securities underwriting, and foreign exchange trading was paramount for their continued business success.

I became the managing director and CIO of Salomon Brothers, one of Wall Street's largest investment banking houses known for being the topmost innovator of any Wall Street firms. Its graduates included Michael Bloomberg and many alumni who became senior advisors to US presidents. Salomon Brothers, along with Goldman Sachs and JPMorgan Chase, were thought of as the crème de la crème of all the Wall Street firms at the time.

Salomon had its own personal reasons for embracing the technological transformation. The firm had a long history of hiring the best and brightest in order to maintain a knowledge gap well above their competitors. What Salomon's senior management soon discovered was that their competitors were investing in new technology as well to close that knowledge gap with Salomon Brothers. None of the investment houses wanted to have any kind of gap in knowledge, speed, or efficiency, so the major thrust in bringing new technology to Wall Street began, and I was ready to revolutionize an industry.

Transforming Trading

Some of the newest hires at Salomon at the time were quantitative analysts who were using high-speed computers to conduct arbitrage trading, a complex series of calculations requiring the simultaneous purchase and sale of an asset in order to profit from the difference.

The speed of these computers was based on the yet-uncommercialized Unix operating system, a platform that heralded immense opportunities for financial services firms on Wall Street and great value to their clients. It came earliest to Salomon Brothers in their proprietary trading organization, and the thought at Salomon was to bring Unix into arbitrage and every other trading platform.

With Unix technology, the firm knew it could not only sustain, but also expand its lead over competition. The firm's technology path became clear and in 1989, I was asked to bring the Unix operating system to the investment firm.

In combination with another new technology called message brokering, Unix provided the company's stock traders and analysts the ability to accomplish tasks that had never been attempted before in trading and to perform those tasks at much higher speeds. Linking Unix to message brokering enabled Salomon to embed computational elements into a data stream before the information even reached a trader's desk.

Prior to that, Salomon traders and analysts used HP calculators to run equations such as price-yield curves—a process that could take up to twenty minutes. By embedding that calculation into the "ticker" information currently streaming into trading desks, traders were now able to make instantaneous decisions on exactly when they should trade blocks of stock. This gave them a twenty- to thirty-minute advantage over everyone else on the trading floor.

In a more profound way, this was the first step in digitizing trading and removing the mystique of the broker. Digitized trading ultimately enabled day traders and individual investors to buy and sell stock and manage their portfolios at their desktops and in their home offices.

Doubling Their Skill Set

I came to Wall Street fresh from my experiences in retention at AT&T, where post divestiture created a frantic need on the part of new competition for technologists with telecommunications experience, and I had the best working for me at AT&T Information Services. It was an interesting parallel, in that my immediate and most pressing challenge was to figure out how I was going to retain the best at Salomon Brothers. This industry was becoming a highly competitive environment with every investment house on Wall Street willing to pay top dollar to attract the best technologists away from Salomon.

I would often tell my people that while they were working for me, they would be implementing the most unique and most competitive set of technologies on Wall Street, and at the end of their segment of their business life with me, they would have developed the skills that would double their marketability. This was the first practice of retention: *increase their marketability by exposing them to the latest technologies*, and Unix was the first proof of that promise.

In order to accelerate the implementation of the operating system, I needed to bring people with Unix expertise into Salomon. I first asked AT&T if I could contract the services of their Unix specialists at Bell Laboratories. Their response was that their policy was not to contract out their brainpower and they would not entertain entering a business arrangement.

In less than a year, I had hired approximately seventy technologists from Bell Labs who either had their hand in developing or were expertly familiar with the Unix operating system. It proved to everyone in the IT organization at

Salomon that the firm was serious about having the most unique set of technologies on Wall Street and that I would keep my promise about doubling the skills and marketability of the technologists there.

From Back Office to Front Office

Before I accepted the position of CIO at Salomon, I learned that technology at the investment firm was considered a "back office" function, using Wall Street vernacular. Back-office people are considered individuals who provide services to the organization such as accounting and human resources. They're not as visible or valued as are the people in the "front office," whose work product is considered by many to be more strategic to the company and its success.

My challenge as an IT leader was to shift the function of the IT organization and their attitudes about themselves from that of a back-office service to one of a front-office, strategic force in the company. This was the second practice of retention that I needed to engage in: *to give them the feeling that their work is strategic to the organization.*

Shifting that reality was the only way to make the company move forward and maintain the knowledge *and* technology gap. I didn't have the time to strategically link the IT organization to the company, as I will discuss later in this chapter. Yet I had to find a way to make my IT organization believe they were indeed front office.

My solution was to make Salomon Brothers' IT organization a stand-alone technology company that would initially sell their Unix-based solutions to Salomon Brothers. After two years, the IT organization would be able to sell their technology products to the entire financial-services industry.

"Where's the 'Money Value'?"

People, especially young people at the onset of their professions, want a sense of belonging and that there's a deeper meaning to the profession they selected and the company for which they work. Immediately after losing a third of my IT organization at AT&T to downsizing and battling back the new competition looking to poach my most-skilled technologists, I leaned on the third practice of retention as the glue to retaining the remainder of my people in the organization: *to create a set of shared values that binds individuals together as one.* Consequently, in one of my first days at Salomon Brothers, I presented my recommended set of values to the entire IT organization.

Standing in front of the thousand employees that comprised the IT group, I wrote out my values on the whiteboard at the front of the room for everyone to see and on which to offer their comments. I had always been a values-based person and always approached my leadership of others through a set of principles and rules. My intent was that everyone would exemplify those values in everything they did and with everyone they engaged with on a day-to-day basis.

I thought that if I enrolled my people in my values, they would be united in values, engaged, loyal to the team and effort, and more productive. I listed my values of communication, collaboration, integrity, and support— the values that had defined and guided the organizations that I led throughout my business life. This being my first engagement on Wall Street and my first exposure to the culture of the industry, I immediately discovered from a question on the floor that my value set was incomplete.

A young man in the middle of the room raised his hand and said, "Mr. Dramis, I don't see 'money' on your list of values."

I replied, "Money is not a value."

The entire organization of one thousand technologists who were just getting to know me erupted in laughter. Over their laughter, the young man shouted, "Mr. Dramis, the reason they're laughing is because this is Wall Street. Money is our only value!"

I realized then that in order to retain these people and make them great, I had to link the "money value" into my set. I believed then, and still believe now, that a values-based organization can become the unique leader in any industry. What we had as an objective at Salomon was to stay unique and become even more so through technology. I needed for this team to remain focused, so I was willing to trade, which happens to be another value on Wall Street.

Since money was a value to them, I added it to my list on the whiteboard and said that if they didn't adopt the values, their bonuses would not be as high as they were in previous years.

Hands began to raise and people spoke out, saying, "You're asking us to be phony. We'll only be honoring the values written out on the whiteboard in order to get our full bonuses."

I responded, "I have great things planned for you, your marketability, and your business lives, but you must support these values. I know that if we communicate with each other, if we collaborate on our projects, if we show integrity in our work and our working relations with teammates and with me, and if we support each other, we will be the most unique IT organization on Wall Street. You will be the most skilled and most marketable technologists in Lower Manhattan or anywhere in the country.

"The incentive I'm using is to tie a large percentage of your bonuses to your living the values that I have up here on the board. I don't care why you're living the values or what motivates you. I just want to see the behavior."

That brings out an interesting point on values. There are values, motivations, and behaviors, but to be honest, I'm not as focused on what is motivating a person as I am on that person's behavior. There many ways to motivate people, such as with money, power, and even emotion. Moreover, motivation is personal and it changes from person to person, and can even change over the course of his or her lifetime. Motivation is important, but I believe it is truly more effective and efficient for a leader to focus on behavior.

In a group of one hundred, one thousand, or ten thousand people, there's going to be a lot of different characters and personalities along with all sorts of drives and motivations. I believe leaders are more effective when they're focusing on the behavior that they want to see in the individual, the team, or the organization. Let the individual's personal motivations get them to that behavior.

My objective was to make the IT organization feel important and unique by being a part of a technological revolution, the depth to which no other Wall Street firm was engaged. And aside from ushering in Unix, I would bind them together with a set of values that would ensure top performance.

The company's IT organization shifted from being a back-office, support function to one of the most valued IT groups on Wall Street. In fact, Salomon Brothers' IT organization was named to the prestigious "*Computerworld* 100" in 1990 as one of the most effective users of information systems in the United States.

Also, many of the people working in the IT organization learned the techniques of leadership, which led several of them to become the CIOs of major institutions across the United States. Institutions such as the Citadel, Merrill

Lynch, Fidelity Investments, and many others were led by people who were in Salomon's IT organization at the time.

After my two-year term with Salomon ended, I met with the firm's senior executives to hold them to their promise of selling the technologies produced by my IT organization to other companies on Wall Street. As I sat there, I reflected on how that promise transformed the mindset of my technologists from being back-office servants to front-office heroes. It was their barrier to exit—their reason for not leaving—and they didn't. It was what encouraged the Unix geniuses to leave Bell Labs and join me at Salomon.

The senior team acknowledged their promise, but then said that the company's profitability gains resulting from the IT products my organization produced changed their minds. They decided to keep the IT group captive and dedicated to the firm, and the IT products we created the intellectual property of Salomon Brothers. As I sat there, I saw the barrier to exit that I had built dissolve before my eyes. Shortly afterward, I exited the position myself.

Nevertheless, my experiences at Salomon Brothers proved that by increasing people's marketability, giving them the feeling that their work is strategic to the organization, and creating a set of shared values that binds individuals together as one does in fact work, even in the most competitive industry in the world.

The Unique Challenges
of Transitional Leadership

After leaving Salomon Brothers, then for a brief time running another company, I founded CIO Strategy, Inc., an IT strategy consultancy that over the next three years was responsible for the technology transformations at Coopers & Lybrand, Citibank, NASDR, and Bankers Trust.

Even though I was the "transitional" CIO for these four companies and not an employed CIO as I was for Salomon Brothers, I still needed to retain the skilled technologists in my organization. This created a unique challenge: how to retain people who, in reality, didn't report to me. I was the consultant, an interim CIO.

When I was at Salomon Brothers, my objective was to make the people in my IT organizations more marketable, and I could keep that promise and accomplish that task. There, I was a full-time employee, I sat at the strategy table, and I had a hand in the transformational technology that was being developed and deployed across the firm. In addition, I was in a full-time leadership position that enabled me to mandate a set of shared values.

I realized that as a transitional leader, I couldn't exercise three of the four practices a leader needs to engage in order to retain skilled technologists. I couldn't make the people working in the IT organization more marketable because my role was to execute the company's technology, not specify the technology that the company should use. I couldn't make them more strategic to the organization since I was not a member of the strategy team.

However, I could reflect the linkage between what they were working on in IT and what was conveyed to me to be the strategy of the organization. Finally, being a transitional leader also eliminated my ability to mandate a set of shared values. All I could do for the people working in IT was to help each of them understand what spending time with me would do for them over the course of their business lives.

As a result of those constraints, I discovered and focused all my efforts on what would become the true secret of retention—the fourth practice of *connecting the work they were engaged in while with me to achieving their personal Business Life Goals.* Over the course of the four assignments, I realized the power of retention when a leader is linked to an individual's **Business Life Goal**.

Coopers & Lybrand— Technology Meets Brain Power

The first company in which I served as a consulting CIO was with Coopers & Lybrand in 1991, an international consultancy that had never had a head of technology. It was a unique opportunity to come into the organization and help the company understand the relationship between technology and the brainpower of their consultants, and the potential and competitive advantage that linkage offered.

I was connected with the top two people in the organization and learned a great deal from each. The first was the vice chair of the board, an amazing person with terrific perspectives and insights into what the firm needed. The second was the chair and CEO, who was serious about shaking up the consulting business as it currently existed. The intersection of these two visionary leaders provided the foundation for the changes that technology would bring to Coopers & Lybrand.

My transitional leadership of the IT organization at Coopers & Lybrand forced me to understand some unique distinctions in the principles of leadership, specifically, how an outside consultant can step in, lead and retain skilled individuals, and encourage great productivity out of them.

For an intermediate entering the scene for a defined period of time then leaving, the traditional relationship between leader and staff is nonexistent. Therefore, all of my efforts had to focus on what I was providing each technologist during that time of transition. My instincts told me that my role, just as it was at Salomon Brothers, was to explain how the work the people were doing would make them more marketable. However, as noted above, I inherited the technology, and although I was transforming the company's technology, I was transforming it into something that the company had selected. I knew what bringing Unix to Salomon Brothers would do for the professions of each technologist there and I could make the promise of doubling their marketability. As an interim leader, making that promise was more challenging.

Nevertheless, I could articulate that the work they were doing was strategic because the tool sets that we were providing the company were creating linkages between the consultancy and technology—linkages that hadn't been established before anywhere. That connection of technology and brainpower was strategic to the company, and the work of the IT group became a critical element in the successful transformation of the company.

The value of the fourth practice of *connecting what technologists are doing in my organization to their Business Life Goals* became very clear to me while at Coopers & Lybrand. There was one particular person in the IT group who was central to carrying out the transformation. I was spending most time with her in deployment and got to know her and her aspirations.

Being both a brilliant technologist and a woman, which was rare at the time for there were not many women in technology, she was continually receiving offers from competition. The only way to retain her was to make the connection for her that the work she was engaged in with me had her squarely on the path to achieving her **Business Life Goal**. That experience formed the practice of linking current tasks to an employee's overall **Business Life Goal**.

Citibank: From International to Global

My next assignment was with Citibank's global bank division in 1993, a global financial institution faced with some unique challenges. They were a well-established international company wanting to become a global company. Let me explain what I mean.

A multinational company is no more than an international company if it's culture is shaped solely by the country in which its headquarters resides. Conversely, a global company is one in which the culture of the country where the regional headquarters is located determines the way business is conducted in that country or region; yet, at the same time, links that local business to a singular global philosophy. Thus, a global company bridges the gap between its centrally located technology and the locally managed business.

In the case of Citibank, the United States was home base and it applied the US culture of business to the bank's regional headquarters and offices across the globe. As a result, there was a constant struggle between Citibank's standards and technology systems in the US and the different standards and technology systems in each operating country.

Transforming the IT organization into a global brand was an interesting challenge, to say the least. Each regional headquarters wanted to maintain its own standards and operating procedures, while Citibank's global-banking headquarters in the US had broader and more purposeful intentions. For example, Citibank wanted the ability to evaluate a multinational client—such as a Ford or Chrysler—as one entity, regardless of the country in which that client was doing business with Citibank.

Take an issue such as credit worthiness. Citibank's global-banking division did not want to evaluate the credit worthiness of the Ford Motor Company of Germany, but rather the credit worthiness of the Ford Motor Company globally. So, the ability to both pull together the information of a global entity such as a Ford or a McDonald's or a Coca-Cola but still be able to service those companies "in country" with in-country standards was very important to Citibank.

The challenge that I had as a transitional leader over that entire IT organization was to meld the cultures of the various people around the world into one integrated technology plan and ensure that the business leaders in each of the locales articulated their needs. Continuing with the example above, the technology plan had to assure that credit risk was still centrally managed while at the same time giving local leaders the flexibility to engage in business with the local branches of that multinational company. The first challenge, which turned out to be a painfully revealing undertaking, was to conduct a technology-road-map-and-gap analysis between the enterprise's current state of technology and their desired state.

Several key people were needed in Citibank's global organization to help bring about this transformative change.

One person, who eventually became the technology leader of the global bank, was a person who had worked for Steve Jobs at NeXT. He was a brilliant, young technologist, but was looking for help in defining his **Business Life Goal**.

I had many discussions with this young man, and through our talks, it became apparent to me that his objective was to become a senior executive, leading either entire businesses or their technology organizations. Through our talks, I also discovered that his experiences were limited to the field of technology itself.

Although his goal was to be a senior executive, he didn't have the experience in leading an organization through a technological transformation, where he had to maneuver through the political pitfalls, contend with cultural differences, and work through any potential resistance. What he needed was experience in dealing with bureaucracies and in melding multiple cultures into a common viewpoint and set of goals.

I explained to him that by working with me on this project, he would learn how to navigate these challenges, just as I had learned over the years, and that he should stay on and learn these skills. That discussion helped me to link that section of his livelihood to his overall **Business Life Goal.**

He stayed and, following his time with Citibank, became one of the most successful IT leaders in the US, becoming CIO of NASDAQ and then of Capital One. That was clearly his intent, and I became an enabler of his professional aspirations through the fourth practice of *connecting what he was doing in my organization to his Business Life Goal.*

NASDR

The National Association of Securities Dealers (NASD) was the self-regulatory organization of the securities industry responsible for the operation and regulation of the NASDAQ stock market. NASDR became the regulatory division of NASD and was ultimately merged with the Financial Industry Regulatory Authority (FINRA) in 2007.

The CEO of NASDR was a brilliant person who went about building the regulatory division as a discrete company in accordance with SEC rulings, which stipulated separating the regulatory arm of NASD from the NASDAQ trading organization.

The issue at hand was that the regulatory branch was "second fiddle" to the exchange part of the organization in technology investments and applications. At the time I was asked to come in as their temporary CIO, their existing broker-registration system was failing badly. I had to build a completely new repertoire of technology, starting with a unique way of registering every broker in the United States.

My interim term started with my ending a two-year-long IT development project and recreating the entire broker-registration system. This reminded me of my start at AT&T Information Services when I had to let go a third of my IT organization in one month. The day I made the announcement of the demise and recreation of the registration system, I was wearing a black trench coat and black fedora. Looking back now, I imagine I was an ominous presence, and the people in the IT organization actually wrote a song about me as the man in black who came in to kill the broker-registration system.

Quite frankly, the IT team that I assembled for the restructuring of the registration system turned out to be some of the best people in technology. They were at a point in their professions where the experience of being there with me at NASDR was a critical stepping-stone in their business life journey.

To complete this assignment, I needed someone to spearhead the technology transformation effort on the days that I wasn't present. At the time, I was a transitional CIO at both Bankers Trust and at NASDR, spending half my week at one company and half at the other. I needed someone to run the organization while I wasn't there, and then I found a key person on the NASDR team whose aspiration was to be a senior executive. Prior to that, he had limited experience in running and managing large teams. The experience he gained as my surrogate when I wasn't there was absolutely critical to his learning the job and acting in the role of a senior leader.

I also needed a leader on the technology side. I found a brilliant technologist on the team whose aspiration was to become an IT leader. But at the time, she was buried in detail work, head down, and working hard in the IT organization. She needed the leadership and project-management skills required to attain her objectives. Having her spearhead the project at NASDR convinced her to stay and also developed her skill sets as an IT leader.

Bankers Trust

When I arrived at Bankers Trust in 1996, the organization had already experienced significant losses in derivatives trading. The trading branch was leaning heavily on the transaction branch to help in its recovery, and the new head of the transactions branch asked me to come in and conduct a technology road map. I needed someone internal to lead the effort.

I connected with a young woman in the IT organization who was in line to become a senior officer, and just as the woman who became the project lead for me at NASDR, this technologist also needed the perspective of leading a large effort in order to be on that path toward achieving her **Business Life Goal**.

While working with her and discussing her ambitions, I discovered that she wanted to become the IT leader at Bankers Trust. I convinced her that leading the technology-road-map process across the various divisions within the transaction branch would provide her with the perspective required to be a senior leader. Even though she was heavily recruited outside the company at that time for her particular technical skills, this opportunity to learn transformational leadership skills encouraged her to stay with me. The road map was an extremely successful plan and became a critical element in facilitating the eventual merger between Bankers Trust and Deutsche Bank.

Investing the Time

In much the same way an organism endures and ultimately thrives by adapting to its environment, being a transitional leader forced me to focus on the fourth practice that would ultimately become the true secret of retention: *connecting what people are doing in the organization to their Business Life Goals.* I invested the time talking with my direct reports and their direct reports to unearth their interests and ambitions. I learned what each of them really wanted to do with their talents and learned skills and accomplishments in their lives.

I was able to guide their understanding through my own experiences and show them that the work they were doing for me was a critical link to achieving their personal goals. That process of communication, discovery, and linkage became my principal method of retaining people when I returned to the full-time position as CIO at BellSouth Corporation.

I think it's really important, though, to dive deeper into the other three practices of retention—marketability, strategic importance, and values—and the experiences each was based on. I provided some examples of them being used at Salomon Brothers and slightly during the four interim assignments. In the next chapter, I will speak to the theory and research that supports each of those three practices and provide examples of each in action.

Chapter 3

What Matters Most

1. Increase their marketability.
2. Instill in them the understanding that they are strategic.
3. Unite and strengthen their efforts through shared values.
4. Connect their work to their **Business Life Goals**.

I believe that these four elements are what matters most to people looking to build their business lives. Although I discovered these while working in the technology industry, it stands to reason that these desires matter most to people—especially young people—working in any industry. If it matters most to them, it should matter most to a leader wanting to retain the best and draw out of them their personal best.

It benefits leaders in any industry to build a practice around each of these elements to retain the people who are already in their organizations and to attract and retain new talent. If the leader is able to do this and meet the needs and expectations of individuals, the four practices become one powerful, comprehensive force in retention.

When people make the connection that the work they are doing is leading edge, strategic, values-driven, and is linked to their business life aspirations, they become extremely loyal to the leader and the organization. I place loyalty to the leader first because, in my experience, many of those whom I have mentored have become lifelong connections, which is the ultimate goal in retention.

The fourth practice of connecting their work to their **Business Life Goals** is the one that requires the leader's utmost attention and deepest involvement. This has the power to create the greatest "stickiness" between the knowledge worker, the leader, and the organization. If while someone is spending time with you, they are actually gaining experiences critical for their meeting their personal business life goals, then they will be incredibly loyal and will not want to move on from your organization.

This chapter will be a deep dive into the first three practices. I will show how each came to being, why it matters so much to people, and how I used each to retain and deeply engage the most-talented employees. In the next chapter, I will share how I was able to bring all four together during my tenure at BellSouth by connecting to the **Business Life Goal** of each of my direct and indirect reports.

Making People More Marketable

At the end of the 1980s, with the demise of cradle-to-grave employment, the concept of job security vanished and the psychological contract between worker and employer was broken for the first time since the end of WWII. What job security meant to people back then was that they would have a job that would pay a decent wage and they were going to be able to provide for themselves and their families until they retired with a pension and social security.

I needed to replace that lost sense of security for the people in my organizations. I believed then, and still do today, that marketability is security, and continuously upgrading and developing marketable skills means more than job security to a person—it means life security.

What matters most to people today, whether they are at the start or in the middle of their business lives, is to become increasingly marketable, and not just by being on top of the latest business practices, but also through the experience of having led organizations (if their aspiration is to become a senior leader).

In a technology organization, change is exponential and the people with talents and skills have to grow their knowledge and experience just as quickly, particularly in companies that use technology as their competitive edge and need to stay ahead of the marketplace with the latest advancements.

For technologists, marketability means gaining knowledge and experience by working on the newest innovations in technology. During my time on Wall Street, the "hot stuff" was the introduction of Unix as a base operating system.

Throughout the history of technology, new, leading-edge innovations have attracted people to companies like moths to a flame. It's a lot like striving to play the most challenging video games. Technologists love technology and love new technology even more.

Tech people are mobile and will move from job to job, just to be involved in the latest technology and to fulfill their insatiable need to keep their skill sets sharp. Few, if any of them, have ever experienced job security, since many only started working in the 1990s. It may seem counterintuitive, but I realized that if I could increase their marketability so they would always be in demand by my competition, they would actually stay, and they did.

The adoption of new technology was critical to the success of the companies that I was a part of and also critical to the marketability of the technologies who worked for me or were assigned. This proved to be a great marriage of corporate and individual need.

Retaining Leaders and Managers

Retaining people by giving them the opportunity to work with the latest innovations and hottest stuff in technology was clearly important, but it didn't end there. Of equal importance to me, and of greater importance in a few instances, was retaining the upcoming leaders of the technology organizations, especially during my interim years with Coopers & Lybrand, Citibank, NASDR, and Bankers Trust.

The ability to lead technologists as a project manager, director, division head, EVP, or CIO is of critical importance to every company in every industry using technology — whether that technology is the product of the company or a support service within the company.

But retaining second- and third-level managers in an organization is another challenge altogether. Beyond their exposure to innovative tools and systems, those whose **Business Life Goals** are to lead organizations or companies needed to acquire leadership experience.

Leadership is, in itself, a marketable element. Learning the latest leadership techniques, how to enroll people in one's vision, and how to unite and engage groups of one hundred, one thousand, or ten thousand through shared values are an even greater marketable asset. Arming first- and second-level managers to become senior leaders with a set of techniques that enable *them* to retain the best talent in their own organizations is ultimately what this book is all about.

My experiences, especially as a transitional leader, led me to understand that teaching leadership techniques was one of the most important elements for helping my direct and indirect reports attain their **Business Life Goals**.

The example I shared earlier about bringing Unix to Salomon Brothers resulted in my second- and third-level managers finding great success in landing bigger and better positions as they advanced in their business lives.

And it wasn't just because they were working with a leading-edge technology, but because of mentoring them in leadership. Several became heads of technology at major corporations such as Merrill Lynch, the Citadel, Fidelity Investments, Bankers Trust, and others.

I recently received an e-mail from a person who worked for me at Salomon Brothers to let me know that he was just named Ernst and Young's Entrepreneur of the Year for 2016. Aside from naming me in an interview as his mentor, he said in the e-mail that I believed in him and taught him things that lead to his "chosen profession and eventual success."

Being a part of the technology transformation of Salomon Brothers and learning to lead the investment firm through that sweeping change made this person far more marketable and, in fact, created a sense of life security for him that is obviously still with him today.

The brilliant female technology supervisor who was central in carrying out the IT transformation at Coopers & Lybrand became more marketable by learning how to manage large technology projects. She went on to become an executive vice president of a technology firm.

I was able to retain that young technology manager at Citibank who had once worked for Steve Jobs at NeXT. His goal was to be a senior executive, but his experience was limited to tool sets and applications and not leadership itself. By staying with me, he learned how to deal with bureaucracies and fuse multiple cultures into a common viewpoint and set of goals. He went on to become the IT leader of Citibank's global-banking division. Following his time with Citibank, he became one of the most successful IT leaders in the US, becoming CIO of NASDAQ and then Capital One.

The young supervisor who spearheaded the technology transformation at NASDR also had a goal of becoming a senior executive, but had limited experience in managing and leading teams. The experience he gained working with me propelled him to become a senior leader in NASD.

The brilliant female technologist I found within the NASDR organization whose aspiration was to be an IT leader stayed with me and developed the leadership and project-management skills required to attain her objectives. She eventually became a departmental CIO at BellSouth with a team of forty people, and then became the CIO at Atlanta Gas Light Company with an organization of over one hundred. She is now the CIO at American Family Insurance Company with several hundred people in her organization.

At Bankers Trust, the young woman I connected with in IT was in line to become a senior officer, but needed the experience of leading a large effort if she was to attain her goal of leading an IT organization. The technology road map that she helped me execute became a critical element in the Bankers Trust-Deutsche Bank merger and propelled her to become the technical executive of that division in Bankers Trust.

All of these individuals, and many others, were able to leverage their proficiencies into extremely secure professions. They stand as testaments to how increasing their marketability by exposing them to innovative technology and mentoring them in leading the company through its transformation put them on the path to achieving their **Business Life Goals**.

Making People Feel More Strategic

In IT, and most likely in other support functions in a company such as accounting, customer care, inventory management, project management, or human resources, it's difficult for people to believe that what they are doing is as critical as the people who are creating the product that their company is marketing.

It is fairly easy for that belief to exist in the minds of the technologists who work in a technology-focused company. As I shared earlier in the case of Telic Corporation, the product that we were working on *was* the product the company was selling. By its very nature, the IT organization was not a support function but rather very strategic to Telic much in the same way the IT organizations at Apple, Google, Microsoft, Oracle, or Facebook are strategic to each of those companies.

Bringing Unix to Salomon Brothers was strategic to the investment firm, yet the IT organization at the time was considered a support function and nothing more. To break through that, I had to essentially create a software product organization. I had to get the technologists to believe, especially the Unix intellects from Bell Labs, that they were joining an Oracle- or Microsoft-like company. That was the reason I was able to retain the individuals who were already a part of the organization from being drawn away by other Wall Street firms. It was also the reason I was able to attract the special talent that I needed from Bell Labs and encourage them to stay with me during my time at Salomon Brothers.

When Salomon changed their intentions of allowing the IT organization to sell the Unix applications as software products to other Wall Street investment firms, not only did I leave, but a number of others in the organization also left shortly afterward.

Once that sense of being a strategic element in the company they were working for was broken, the brightest minds were moving on to other companies. This speaks to how tenuous this relationship is for someone looking to be valued and how quickly that link with the heart and mind of the employee can be broken. That proved to me that that the feeling of importance was absolutely critical to retaining people.

Here's a perfect example: After I left, my head of networking immediately quit to lead technology at UUNET, one of the first and largest commercial Internet service providers at the time and one of the early tier-one networks. That company was right out there on the leading edge of technology and very strategic to global communication and commerce, and he wanted his work to be strategic and meaningful, not to be considered a support function buried away in some corner of the company.

I had influenced him to come from the military sector, where he was heading up military networks to what he thought was going to be a competitive, technology-selling company. When that didn't pan out, he left to join one. Others left to join technology-focused companies as well.

As a transitional leader, I discovered that it was far more challenging to have the people in a supporting organization believe that the work that they were doing truly was strategic. That required communicating the business objectives and strategy of the corporation to the IT organization and having the technologists understand that their work was the key to making that strategy happen and allowing the corporation to achieve their business objectives.

In the case of Citibank, the strategy was to create a global bank. The technology to make that happen had to be uniformly deployed but locally managed. That was not only articulated by me, the transitional leader, but also by that very gifted woman who lead the global bank's operations at the time.

I believe that in any organization, people themselves have to believe that they are of critical importance and not just a bureaucratic function or a replaceable commodity. The challenge is difficult when technology is an enabler of other business functions and not the main thrust of the enterprise, but there are ways of instilling that sense of importance. The most effective is by having the senior leadership of the company articulate the linkage between what the technology people are working on and the business strategy of the company, and how the IT organization is essential to making that strategy a reality.

I found that communication from senior leadership to their employees was vital in each of the transitional jobs that I held, and I was fortunate to have the vice chair of Coopers & Lybrand, the EVP of Citibank, the EVP of Bankers Trust, and the CEO of NASDR communicate that linkage to each of their respective IT organizations.

Values-Based

People tend to prefer working with people that they like and can get along with. This is as much a condition for staying with a company as anything else. They feel bonded together through a set of shared attitudes and beliefs such as communication, collaboration, and integrity. In my experience, the organizations that were most successful always seemed to have a certain "people chemistry." They seemed to do more things together. They may have been fairly diverse groups both ethnically and economically, but they seemed to gel together really well. I believe this is especially important to young people today and can be a strategy in retaining them. I believe that working in an organization that has a set of shared values as its guiding principles creates a sense of security and belonging.

A number of years ago, I realized that what brings people together is a set of shared values—people who have the same passion for the same type of things. If their work mattered to each of them, and if the projects they were working on were of importance to them, they felt collectively aligned to others in the organization. Later on in my business life, I found out that there is a great deal of research that supports the fact that having a set of shared values in common does often lead to organizational success.

A few years ago, a Gartner study focused on what elements contribute to the building of high-performance organizations. In that study, they discovered that each of the high-performance organizations they evaluated had five similar characteristics: shared values, ambitious goals, focus and alignment, organizational agility, and a shared business model.[20]

Values-based organizations are continually in the lead. Jim Collins and Jerry Porras, in their study about visionary companies, stated that many of the most successful companies adhere to a set of principles called "core values," the guiding principles that prescribe behavior and action. Core values help people distinguish right from wrong, and they can help companies determine if they are on the right path and fulfilling their business goal. They found that companies that are formed around core values have outperformed the stock market in the US by a factor of twelve since 1925.[21]

Before developing a values-based organization, however, it is important that the IT leaders commit themselves to going the full distance. If a leader starts down the path of being a values-based organization, they have to make sure that they and everyone in the organization will walk the talk. Patrick Lencioni wrote in *Harvard Business Review* that "empty value statements create cynical and dispirited employees, alienate customers, and undermine managerial credibility."[22]

As an example, consider this value statement taken from a company's annual report: "We treat others as we would like to be treated ourselves. We do not tolerate abusive or disrespectful treatment. We work with customers and prospects openly, honestly, and sincerely. Our corporate values are communication, respect, integrity, and excellence." Sounds great, right? Well, this particular company posted that value statement but didn't live by it. The result was one of the largest financial meltdowns in history. The company? Enron Corporation.[23]

Like anything else, there is a process for developing values-based organizations, and it is very straightforward. These are the three steps and the definition of each of the three teams that should be tasked with disseminating the values and ensuring their adherence.

Step 1: Every organization has values. The hard part is to articulate those values and make sure everyone in the organization knows them. The first step is to have a process for determining what the organization's values are, incorporate those values through business processes, and implement an intervention process to make sure that those values are demonstrated in how people work and engage with each other.

Step 2: In order make values real, they have to be linked into the business objectives. If a company says it's a "people organization" but never meets as a group to discuss people and put together a development process, the company and its leaders and employees are not walking the talk. There has to be oversight processes to make sure that the values are aligned. If integrity is a value that the IT leader wants the organization to support, then there needs to be a "whistleblower" process in the organization, and there need to be examples given of what integrity is or is not.

The values-determination process can create real pain within a company. Let me give you an example. If "inclusion" is a value for the organization, and the best person (scientist, engineer, project manager) in the organization is someone who just doesn't deal with people very well, does that person stay or not? If inclusion is a value, and collaboration is a value, that person who doesn't buy into those values can't remain, even though their contributions may be pretty high. That's painful, but a lesson to everyone how serious the leader is about everyone living the values.

Step 3: The third step in creating a values-based organization is an intervention process that ensures the values are being lived out in the ways the leader has established. This process starts by giving the role of managing the values to a specific group of people. Most organizations have three distinct teams to accomplish that effort: the strategy team, the core team, and the business team.

The strategy team includes the people who report directly to the CIO. They are responsible for orienting the organization to its external environment—to understand what is happening in the marketplace, how the objectives of the organization are linked into technical projects, and what the competitive marketplace is. It is their responsibility to create processes that engage the technology organization with the business, and to link up with the technology-road-map process to help transform the organization.

The core team, however, is really the key element in a values-based organization. The core team consists of the people reporting to the strategy team members who are themselves managers of people. The core team also includes the strategy team members. The job of the core team—as it relates to the values—is to define and maintain a work environment that is aligned to the values and to create processes that support the values. Their role is also to ensure that the members of the organization adhere to the values as a condition of staying within the organization.

The business team is the last team, and everyone else is essentially on that team. Everyone is ultimately responsible for producing the products and services provided by the organization to the marketplace, and to do so according to the stated values.

As I mentioned earlier, one of the most important elements is to create processes that allow for values to be part of the objectives of an organization. The best way I can describe this is to mention the experience I had at BellSouth. The company adopted five core values as part of its basic platform of values. The values were a belief in people, integrity, excellence in customer service, community focus, and communication.

We decided that the best way to ensure that the values were translated into the way we did business was to make sure the core team understood each of those values. We decided to have the entire core team (all 250 of them) meet one day each month to discuss what the values were and how those values applied to our way of doing work. We brought in outside speakers, we challenged the organization to articulate different scenarios where values came into play, and we talked about the actions that the organization needed to take in supporting and adhering to the values.

In this process, we made each monthly session dedicated to one particular value. In the meeting for the value of community focus, we decided that the best way to convey it was to go out and actually do community service. So when this came up twice a year, we went out and built houses for underprivileged people in the Atlanta area through Habitat for Humanity. During the six years that we went through this process of living the values, we were able to build nineteen different houses. All 250 of us went out and built these homes.

It's important to live the values through a defined process. I always had the value of communication as a core part of every organization that I have been a part of. To walk the talk in communication, I developed a process wherein each member of my direct reports (the strategy team) would meet with me once a week, and they would discuss with me the two most important items on their list of activities.

For the communication value, we talked specifically about communication techniques and disciplines and developed a process of ensuring that open communication was observed in all of our day-to-day processes. For example, at each of our weekly strategy team meetings, we discussed the two most important items that were on the plate for each of the groups represented by the strategy team members. Our objective was to disseminate that information to every single person in the organization. We wanted to treat everyone as members of the organization in terms of information flow.

After we had communicated the top-two items for each group to the whole organization, I would call a random person in the organization to see if they received the information.

At one of my organizations, we had several hundred people working in international locations—a couple hundred in Japan, and a couple hundred in the UK. (I learned a valuable cultural lesson in this exercise.) I picked a name from the organization chart and would call them randomly and ask them if they could recite to me part of the list of the things that were discussed at the strategy team meeting and disseminated to them.

After conducting this calling program for about four or five weeks, I received a panicked call from my direct report running our Japanese IT organization at the time. He was begging me to stop calling people and quizzing them. He revealed that if the person on the phone didn't know the answer to my question, they would be embarrassed and lose face and contemplate resigning.

He told me that he had talked two people out of quitting in the first three weeks of the program. This was a timely insight for me, and I changed my approach from that day on. Going forward, I would have my secretary pre-call the person, tell him or her that I was going to call, and instead of rewarding the person only when they were able to answer the question, I would send a little gift to them just for participating.

A similar instance happened in the UK (but on the opposite end of the spectrum). When someone was able to answer my questions, they would be so teased by their peers that they did not want the prize. So we had to change it for the UK also, from a prize for getting it "right" to just a prize for participating. It's important for leaders to know the cultural dynamics in running a global organization are important when they start putting the values into practice, especially the value of communication.

It is also important that every individual in the organization lives by those values and for the leader to let it be known that there will be no equivocation. Let me give you an example. One of my key employees of one of my companies did not want to attend my staff meetings. He thought that he was not able to communicate. He ran about 30 percent of my organization. After multiple attempts to get him to attend to share what he was doing with the rest of the staff, I had to let him go, even though he was supervising a very critical piece of my organization.

I will be speaking more to values in Chapter Four during my BellSouth years, and you can also find more information on creating values-based organizations in my book *The CIO Handbook*.

Discovering the Secret to Retention

In this competitive market for skilled people loyal to themselves and not to any one company, IT leaders—all leaders for that matter—need an edge. I discovered that edge by learning what matters most to people: to become more marketable, to be considered strategic to the company, and to feel included and a part of something by working under a set of shared values.

When the fourth practice of connecting the work people are engaged in to their **Business Life Goals**, the four practices are harmoniously linked and the IT leader will have discovered the true and most comprehensive secret to retention.

My experience at Salomon Brothers and in the four transitional assignments on Wall Street provided the foundation for my return to telecommunications as the chief information, ecommerce, and security officer for BellSouth Corporation. There, I was able to apply and perfect all four practices of retention and ultimately connect with the **Business Life Goals** of my direct and indirect reports. That process of blending all four practices is what I will now share in Chapter Four.

Chapter 4

From Job Security to Life Security

It had been a number of years since I last worked in the telecommunications industry, and coming back as the executive vice president, CIO, and security officer for BellSouth was hugely energizing for me in two ways.

I was bringing to bear ten years of experience as a transitional leader, transforming IT organizations in one of the most competitive industries in the world, and I was bringing a tested practice in retaining skill technologists and technology leaders during one of the most inventive and vibrant times in technology.

In that time, I have been able to maximize the effect and outcome of each of the three practices of retention. At BellSouth, I could help those in the IT organization become more marketable, for my role was to not only execute the company's technology, but to specify the technology being used.

I could also make the organization more strategic to the company as a member of the strategy team. This meant that I could now connect what the people were doing in the IT organization to their **Business Life Goals**.

Most importantly, I could bring all four practices of retention together by connecting to the **Business Life Goal** of each of my direct and indirect reports. When people make the connection with the work they are doing to their long-term **Business Life Goals**, they become very loyal to the organization they're engaged with, and the four practices become one powerful force in retention.

Prior to my joining BellSouth, the company did not have a CIO. They had individual IT leaders in each of the various divisions, but not a corporate-level CIO. In 1998, a new and visionary CEO created that corporate-level position to link together the disconnected parts of the company, fragmented as a result of the AT&T divesture.

When I first interviewed at BellSouth, I thought it would be another transitional assignment. I soon discovered that BellSouth's intent was to make the job of corporate CIO a permanent position. In an unplanned way, I became that long-term CIO in a company that was itself going through a technological reformation. They needed to conduct a technology evaluation and implementation plan similar to the ones I executed at Citibank and Bankers Trust. I was in familiar territory, to say the least.

My first effort was to bring the entire company through a process that I detail in my first book, *The CIO Handbook*— a process I call the "Technology Road Map." This is essentially a gap analysis between the current state of a company's technology and the desired state needed to support the company's business processes and future business strategy. Equally critical to this road-map process is an effective transition plan that transitions the company from current-state technology to desired state.

One caveat that makes the process even more challenging is that the CEO and business leaders must lead the process, not the IT organization. This means that the entire process requires the sponsorship and involvement of the CEO who is the ultimate recipient of the technology road-map and implementation plan.

A CEO running a business needs to have a grasp of all the strategic assets that are employed by his or her company. If technology is a key element of a company's success, then technology needs to be governed like any other strategic asset.

At the end of BellSouth's road-map process, which lasted roughly eight months, it was time to form an IT organization to lead the company through its transition and into its desired state of technology.

This was also my chance to engage all four practices of retention at once and to their fullest extent. The technology plan that emerged from the road-map process would require leading-edge technology to run the company. Aside from the huge value it was bringing to the company, it also meant that I could begin working closely with my direct and indirect reports to unfold their **Business Life Goals** and plan out their **Business Life Segments** during my ten-year tenure with BellSouth.

Becoming More Marketable

To meet the objectives of the company, we had to install, for one of the first times in telecommunications history, a comprehensive middleware layer that I named the "Message Broker Databus." It allowed us to connect to BellSouth's nine thousand legacy systems and enabled us to create the type of client-server applications that were being deployed across other industries.

It also enabled us to connect our various databases, where for the first time we needed to understand that the same customer who was ordering basic telephone service and wireless service was also the same customer ordering DSL service. It was critical to get all of those three data elements linked through a middleware layer. This forced the IT organization to learn some of the most leading-edge practices currently being deployed in technology.

In working with new middleware technologies, the people in the IT organization became increasingly more marketable to the telecommunications industry as well as to other industries. Moreover, this was the advent of BellSouth's Internet-enabled practices. As a result, I was named the head of e-commerce and tasked with creating an eStore and developing an overall interactive company experience.

All of these new technologies and ensuing business strategies were just beginning to emerge in the telecommunications industry. This forced us to hire outside people to lead the middleware- and Internet-based transformations. We also had to educate people inside the organization and bring them to realize that customers would, for the first time, be interacting directly with the company through online means—an interaction that was once the exclusive domain of the company's call centers.

This was essentially a breakthrough transition for Bell-South. That extension of our core business to our customers through the Internet required us to look at our technology in a different way and to pepper the organization with outside talent who could accelerate our learning curve.

What also increased the marketability of people in the BellSouth IT organization was that the multimillion-dollar effort to herald in new technology required unique project-management and leadership skills. The specialized talent that I was bringing into the organization to lead the transformation needed to have project-management skills. And my training them and having them lead a technology road map would enhance their leadership skill set and enable them to become more marketable as well.

In fact, five people that were part of the organization at the time are today CIOs or senior leaders of other major organizations throughout the world. The CIO for Liberty Mutual, the head of applications development at Liberty Mutual, the CIO of Family Home Insurance, and the CTO for Capital One were all members of my organization at the time.

Being Strategic to the Company

Earlier in the book, I shared how I was able to make the technologists at Salomon Brothers feel more strategic to the organization by creating a separate technology subsidiary tasked with creating technology products for the investment firm. The IT organization at BellSouth was not a separate entity, but rather a support function within the company. To make this organization become more strategic required me to be an active member of the chairman's council and to sit at the strategy table of the company. My ability to articulate its business strategy and link that into the individual activities in the technology transformation was key to getting all people—both full time and consultants, all ten thousand of them—linked into the strategy.

I accomplished this by holding "State of the Business" meetings twice a year with all ten thousand people in the IT organization: five thousand in Birmingham, Alabama, and five thousand in Atlanta, Georgia. Not only would I communicate our objectives, but the CEO and other business leaders at BellSouth would come to those meetings as well and talk about the objectives of the company. They would explain how they were using the technology produced by the IT organization to achieve their business objectives. Everyone in the organization knew that what he or she was doing was very instrumental and critical to the success of the company.

For example, it was vital for the company to be Internet enabled. It was their desired state of technology across the enterprise and as quickly and creatively as possible. We called it "e-tizing." Each of the business units of BellSouth had an e-tizing objective, which was then shared at each business meeting and linkages were made to what the IT organization was actually doing to support each business unit achieving their "e-tizing" objective.

Another example of being strategic to the organization was in bringing in long distance, given that local Bell-operating companies were given permission to provide long distance to their customers. Each person's role in the organization in bringing BellSouth into long distance was articulated in those meetings in Atlanta and Birmingham. Every person in the IT organization understood the Bell-South business strategy, the IT organization's objectives, and their essential roll in linking those two.

Shared Values

The third practice of uniting and strengthening the organization's efforts through shared values now came into play in a most timely and impactful way. One of the values at BellSouth at the time was collaboration, and we were going through a period of earnings issues and had to cut costs. As with any major company, BellSouth was cutting what they believed to be spurious costs. So one of the rules that went out was that the company would no longer be providing coffee or pastries at meetings. I gave this as an issue for my core team to resolve, and what they decided to do was for every single meeting held by anyone in the IT organization, the team or department that was sponsoring the meeting would provide the refreshments, but they had to provide them in a unique way.

Since we wanted to invest in people, we decided that we would suspend cynicism for the company cutting out coffee and pastries and find a creative way to "have our cake and eat it too." We came up with the idea of a bake sale. Each of the teams in the organization would take turns sponsoring the sale for each meeting with all the profits going to charity. That first year, we ended up donating $30,000 from bake sales alone.

In terms of the integrity value, we had people from our compliance organization within the company and specialists from the outside come in and talk with us about having and displaying integrity. We talked about the benefits of integrity and the penalties and pitfalls organizations face in the absence of integrity and honesty.

Creating values or living the values expressed by the company is a long and difficult process, but well worth the time investment. It takes at least a year to articulate the values and have people understand what the implications are for working in a values-based organization. The values then have to be worked into all business processes. One day a month then committed to just talk about values—a costly undertaking for a busy organization leading the company's technological revolution. Yet those monthly meetings actually kept us united and strengthened our efforts.

Linking to *Business Life Goals*

In my transitional leadership positions, I had my first glimpse of the retention power of just linking informally to the **Business Life Goals** of the individuals assigned to me. At BellSouth, as a permanent IT leader, I was able to create a very formal process for understanding the **Business Life Goal** of every one of my direct reports and those who worked directly for them. And over the course of my ten years with the telecommunications company, I would take on the role of **Business Life Mentor** to each one of them.

Linking to a person's **Business Life Goal** became the most important retention practice that I could ever have engaged in, and I recommend that every leader in any industry engage in that practice. It is the true secret of retention, for it's the stickiest part of any retention program. Although time consuming, linking to their **Business Life Goals** was very beneficial to my direct and indirect reports, not only for the time they spent with me while at BellSouth, but for the years following where they remained connected to me to continue to learn and grow.

I learned that life security meant more than making my reports more marketable; I learned that mentoring them in their leadership journey truly gave them life security.

At the end of the day, success is a function of retaining the correct people in the organization. The awards listed below are ones that were given to the BellSouth organization during my tenure with the company.

- *Computerworld*'s 100 Best Places to Work in IT (five years running)
- Top 10 in Diversity category: *Computerworld*'s 100 Best Places to Work in IT
- SecurE-Biz Leadership Award
- InformationWeek 500 Most Innovative Users of Technology
- *CIO* magazine's Enterprise Value Award

Chapter 5

The Real Secret of Retention—Business Life Goals

I have often thought about the factors that led to the success of the IT organizations that I led in the 1990s and 2000s during my Wall Street years with Salomon Brothers and in my telephone, e-commerce, and security years with BellSouth. I found that in each instance, I was able to link into the business life of the individuals who comprised those organizations.

I learned that a leader's first job is to connect in the deepest way possible to their direct and indirect reports. And I learned the power of the fourth practice of retention—connecting their work to their **Business Life Goals**.

Being on the path to their **Business Life Goals** is all about helping them accumulate the skills, relationships, knowledge, and education that help them attain their professional aspirations. If a leader can link an individual's current job to his or her **Business Life Goal**, then that person coming to work every day also comes to realize that what they are doing is relevant and purposeful to their future, not just to today. They realize that they are working there because they are engaged in a work project or leadership experience that will keep them on the path toward their goal. That's a hugely powerful connection for people—especially young people—to make.

This is why I believe leadership starts with the individual. The first area that leaders must focus on is their relationship as mentor to their direct reports and to the people who report to their direct reports.

In my experience, the first thing a leader has to do is fill the gap in what's missing inside those individuals— what they may be lacking and need in order to advance in their professions. What's missing in one person, such as humor, drive, attention to detail, or technical depth, may not be missing in another. So a leader must have a genuine way to connect with each individual to discover what their goals are and what gaps need to be filled so each can realize and achieve their own unique aspirations.

I believe the role of a leader today is to unearth their direct and indirect reports' **Business Life Goals** from their thought processes, and make it tangible and visible for them. For this reason, I formulated a mentoring process to help people think through what would have them feel fulfilled at the end of their business life and how to programmatically chart a path comprised of **Business Life Segments** that makes that end point of fulfillment tangible and possible. We'll cover the process of helping people develop their **Business Life Plan** and define their segments a little later on in this chapter.

First, leaders must be prepared to help mentor their direct and indirect reports in defining their **Business Life Goals**, a difficult process for someone in their late twenties or in their thirties that truly requires the perspective of a senior leader.

Over the course of my business life, I have discovered how difficult it is for people to fast-forward into their future and imagine the setting and situation that will encompass the last day of their job. Everyone wants to make the right decisions and choices in their business life, but they often have no context within which to frame those choices. They want the jobs that they are engaged in to contribute to their professional goals, but so few actually go through the process of planning out their business life with detail and discipline.

Having context means people have an understanding of the arc of their business life and where their achievements will ultimately carry them. So to encounter no regrets along the way, they have to make purposeful choices. If they have a **Business Life Goal** and they plan to achieve that goal, then all the decisions they make along the way will be directionally correct for them.

Their goal should be to direct their profession based on an underlying set of personal values that they, along with the coaching and mentoring of a leader, unearth by reflecting on what *they* desire the end of their business life to look and feel like.

The End-of-Business-Life Paragraph: A Backward Process

What helps leaders mentor this process is that a person's ability to envision his or her life and profession is a backward process rather than a forward one. Starting at the end means that they will need to put a lot of thought into knowing what will make their intervening years intentional and, as a result, more fulfilling. If they want to experience a purposeful life and livelihood, they have to create and pursue a long-term strategy.

If a leader's direct and indirect reports structure their decision making by reflecting on their end point and working their way back to the present, the decisions that they make along the way will give them greater control over their lives. Their **Business Life Plan** will help guide their choices and will result in a more fulfilling business life with fewer regrets for having possibly missed something while on their journey.

In my mentoring engagements with clients from all walks of life, I ask individuals to reflect on the future and what they truly want to be doing at the end of their work life. I ask them to describe the scene and define what it is they are physically engaged in. I find it helpful for them to describe that last day as a journal entry, or **End-of-Business-Life Paragraph**. They soon discover that this is not an easy task.

What I learned early on is that, in the first draft of their paragraph, many make the mistake of defining their job function or their day-to-day responsibilities. That is not the objective of this exercise. There are a couple of constraints that I put on people writing their paragraph. The first is that they cannot describe a *job*—they have to describe what they are *doing*. The second thing is that what they are doing has to be so important and impactful that, as they are doing it on that last day, they know that time spent—the sacrifices that they made, the positions that they took, the education that they underwent—was all worthwhile. The intent is for your people to write about their feelings, their sense of accomplishment, and their sense of fulfillment on that last day.

As I noted earlier, it's a difficult process for someone in their late twenties or thirties to think forty years forward. Many will over- or underinflate their dreams. People at the onset of their business life are unable to write an effective life plan alone. I believe that period in a young person's job is no more than an extension of their college education.

It's a time for them to understand what the world is all about, understand what life is all about, and start to think about the things that really matter in their lives. At the end of their twenties and into their thirties, developing **Business Life Goals** becomes more realistic, but to do so requires them to start deliberately choosing the destinations they want and start considering the end point of their business life.

I mentioned earlier that it's not a "job function" that the leader is asking their direct and indirect reports to write about. The goal is to have each individual describe what he or she is physically doing on that last day and to describe the thoughts that they are having in reflecting over the course of their professional life that got them to this point in the future.

The Last Day of the Last Job

The leader can begin the process by sharing these examples of **End-of-Business-Life Paragraphs** with each of his or her direct and indirect reports, or having them read my book *Creating an Intentional Life*. Have them write a first draft of their **End-of-Business-Life Paragraph** and see what it looks like. Encourage them to put effort into making it meaningful. Ask them to write it so that—by their description—the next twenty or thirty years feel as if they were worthwhile based on what they were doing.

After writing the first draft of their **End-of-Business-Life Paragraph**, the leader should review it with each individual, scrubbing it of title and positional descriptions. Often, people start with a position held rather than what they are doing on their last day. In most cases, the leader will have to go through three or four revisions of the paragraph until his or her reports start talking about what they will actually be doing and why it's meaningful to them.

Once the person's paragraph is fully fleshed out, he or she is ready for the next step. The process of identifying the underlying business position that enables the paragraph entry to come true involves answering certain questions.

For example, one mentee said that on his last day he was attending a ceremony for the dedication of a community center in his name.

The question would then be, "How was the name decided upon for the building?" Was it because of that person's participation in the community, and they were honoring the person because of their outstanding community work? Or was it because the person made a large donation?

If it was from work in the community, then a **Business Life Plan** would be developed that was associated with all the work that somebody would be doing between now and then in their community. It would include positions along the way that gave the person the skills required. If it were associated with dollars that were provided as a donation, then that's a different path. The leader would then discuss with the individual about what size the building was, how many dollars they think were involved, and what type of position would have enabled that person to have accumulated the income to be able to make the donation for something like that in the first place.

Leading toward a Different Ending

Sometimes as people dive in and reflect deeply on their **End-of-Business-Life Paragraph**, they find they need to make a profound shift. For example, one person, after writing a traditional "I want to be at the top of a corporation" paragraph, really thought about it and decided that it would not, in the end, be meaningful for her.

When she started talking about the things that she *wanted* to do, they were all around influencing people spiritually through reading books that held an important place in her life. Once we found that out, we defined a **Business Life Goal**—the owner of a Christian bookstore.

The job that she happened to have at the time was as a project manager in the IT organization. Initially, it was hard to see how to get from her current position to that end point of owning and running a Christian bookstore. But there are subtle steps that a person can take that will enable them to get to that final stage.

In order for this particular person to begin her journey, she had to start teaching a Christian learning class on Saturdays and Sundays. To do that, she had to have her weekends free. Her current job did not allow her free weekends, so she had to look for a position within the organization that was more structured around a nine-to-five, Monday-through-Friday schedule. She applied for and obtained a position in charge of processes and procedures. This was a very difficult position to attract people to because it required a lot of writing and was less exotic and less deadline oriented. But it needed to be done. Once she realized that that position was really an enabling position for her because it would free up her weekends, she became one of the best process documenters that the company had ever had.

The mentoring process that I brought people through included my checking back with them each month for the first two quarters, and then once every quarter following the first two. After the first three or four months, I found that this individual had started teaching a class on Christian learning. In checking back with her two quarters later, I found that she had purchased some books to augment her courseware and began building a small library of books. Two quarters after that, I discovered that she had been asked by a student in her class about the books that they were reading, and whether or not she could help them obtain the books.

When I last checked, that small library of books expanded to include copies that were available for purchase by her students. It continued to grow, and she had the beginnings of her Christian bookstore.

The Incentive to Succeed

Another mentee had just become CEO of a company that was owned by her husband who suddenly passed away. She had no professional training in running a company, and was questioning how she would be able to make the necessary changes in her life and go through the necessary learning curve to be able to be an effective CEO. When we discussed her **End-of-Business-Life Paragraph**, we discovered a lot of elements around helping communities.

As we unearthed the position that allowed her paragraph to be written, we came to the conclusion that being the chairperson of the United Way for a major metropolitan area would be a good match. However, in order for people to be selected to chair organizations such as the United Way, they had to be a successful businessperson, educator, or government leader with a proven track record.

That knowledge provided all the incentive she needed to become a successful CEO over the course of the next five years. She took courses and read books to improve every facet of her job from leadership skills to presentation skills. As of my last contact with her, her company was doing increasing well and she was currently serving on select United Way committees. She was well on her path toward the chairperson role that she desired.

Here are some additional examples of **End-of-Business-Life Paragraphs**:

- One person wrote that he was sitting at his desk, putting the last few keepsakes in boxes that he would take to the next phase of his life. With each one that he placed in the box, he was thinking about the people and the projects that each memento represented. He felt so privileged to have known so many talented people. In the process of doing that, his assistant interrupted him to remind him of a few more appointments right after lunch. At one of those appointments, he was going to hand over the reins of his current position to someone else. He wrote how his entire team was excited about their accomplishments and the changing leadership.

- A woman began her **End-of-Business-Life Paragraph** by explaining why she was so happy on the last day of her business life. Most people would think that her excitement was because her job was ending, but it wasn't that. The schedule of that last month was filled with the types of challenges that at one time had been a source of frustration, but now were a source of pride for overcoming them. She believed that at her retirement party, people were going to say that she drove people to accomplish more than they thought they could, with high expectations for them and for herself. She felt that people believed that she was a true mentor who impacted people in their business lives, regardless of their level. She hoped that she would be thought of as a leader whose focus was always on what was in the best interest of the business, not driven by a personal agenda.

- Another described in his **End-of-Business-Life Paragraph** that he would be walking out the door of his office complex, getting in his car, and heading home to start an around-the-world trip with his spouse for some much-deserved rest and relaxation void of demands and deadlines. Then, he wanted to begin working in his boutique wine shop.

Each of these and other **End-of-Business-Life Paragraphs** described a position or avenue that was significantly different than what each person was working on at the time. The path from where they were at the moment to where they wanted to be was filled with steps that had to be accomplished, such as education, skill development, and relationship building. That essentially outlined their **Business Life Plan**, an instrumental tool that will be explained later in the chapter where we discuss such accomplishments as **Business Life Segments.**

As I shared at the onset, putting direct and indirect reports on the path to their **Business Life Goals** is really all about helping them amass the skills, relationships, and knowledge that will help them attain their goals. The key is for the leader to link their direct and indirect reports' current jobs with their **Business Life Goals**, and help them realize that what they are doing is relevant and necessary.

Helping employees define their **Business Life Goal** and linking their current activities to their end-of-business-life aspirations is the beginning of the process. To define one's **Business Life Goal**, an individual must first develop a **Business Life Plan**. Such a plan consists of three-year **Business Life Segments** working backward from their

Business Life Goal to the present day. Each of these **Business Life Segments** has the skills and experiences required for them to reach the next segment and ultimately their **Business Life Goal**.

To continue the process, the leader must spend time with their people to help them construct their **Business Life Plans**. The overall benefit of the **Business Life Plan** and **Business Life Segment**–development process is that the answer to the question "what do I do next?" is clearly revealed. It becomes evident to the individual that the best solution is to obtain the skills, secure the relationships, and gain the education and experiences required for the next segment.

By replacing the traditional career-planning process with the stepladder approach of **Business Life Segments**, the leader exercises another principle in the Four Secrets of Retention: creating a greater life security for his or her reports and a stronger guarantee of personal and professional success than the job-security approach could ever offer.

The Business Life Plan

Once the leader has helped his or her reports unearth their **Business Life Goals**, the real stickiness in the Four Secrets of Retention comes from the leader investing further time helping individuals develop a **Business Life Plan**.

I have found that one of the best and most educational ways to do that is to ask the individual to research at least three people who have held or currently hold a position of a similar nature and then research the education, skills, and jobs that led those three people to their current positions. Those educational elements, experiences, and jobs are then partitioned into three-year **Business Life Segments**, and the **Business Life Plan** is then developed and in full view from that exercise.

In my life, I have discovered that if a business professional is going through the process of acquiring skills, taking a new job, or pursuing a new profession, his or her business life is typically patterned into three-year **Business Life Segments**. The first year is the learning period, the second year is when the individual implements his or her contributions and changes, and part of the third year is the time they evaluate their results and achievements.

It also follows that two to three years would be the amount of time needed to obtain a post-graduate degree or PhD, if the person's end-of-business-life position requires that level of education. The next step in this process requires the person to consider the segments still available before retirement.

Once an individual's end-of-business-life position is defined and he or she determines the age at which they would like to retire, they then have to measure three-year segments working backward to where they are today. For instance, if a person is thirty-three years old and looking to retire at fifty-four, they have seven actionable segments—or viable decision points—to get the education, acquire the skills, attain the positions, and accomplish the things necessary to obtain their end goal—the position you as their leader helped them unearth in their **End-of-Business-Life Paragraph**.

Let me share how this process of researching three people who currently hold a similar position worked for one particular person. His **End-of-Business-Life Paragraph** had him making a presentation at the National Science Foundation. In his fact-finding, he discovered that the people who held similar positions and made presentations to the National Science Foundation had either a PhD or had achieved significant accomplishments in the field and practice of science.

One of the three people he researched was a lead technical partner in a venture firm. Further research then revealed a composite of the position that he would have to hold three years prior to the day of the presentation, then three years before that position, then three years prior to that.

As he worked all the way back to the present, he noted all the skills and positions that were required to achieve each level along the way, ultimately resulting in a position as lead technical partner making a presentation at the National Science Foundation. As he looked at these positions and worked it back to his current position, he realized that the three-year segments required him to move from the technical architecture field to being a consultant, then one of the leading consultants. From that point, he would need to join a venture firm as an associate and then advance to partner and then to lead technical partner.

Once he had these necessary segments filled in, he looked at the skills that were required to accomplish each of the segments. In order to be an effective consultant to start him off on his journey, he needed to be more adept at presentations and needed to start publishing some of his thoughts. He took the necessary courses to make him an effective presenter, and began submitting articles to technical journals.

Checking back with him after a couple of years, I found that he had moved on to being a consultant, and I was pleasantly surprised to find that, about four years after we started this whole process, he was listed on the front page of a technical magazine as one of the top four technical consultants in the country. At my last check, he had joined a venture firm and was working his way up the ranks toward the position of lead technical partner.

The leader begins to realize that partitioning their peoples' lives into these segments can really help them make business-life decisions. It will keep them focused on those experiences and skills that are required to link each of their three-year segments to the next.

Uncovering the biographies of the people who are occupying or have occupied the position they are interested in is a valuable tool in helping people model their position of interest. Encourage your direct and indirect reports to dig out the life path of those individuals. Create a composite of their backgrounds, and your people will have a general idea of what steps they will have to take, the paths they will have to follow, and the three-year action segments they will have to complete in order to arrive at that position they desire in the future.

I believe helping people model their position in this fashion is a critically important undertaking, for it helps individuals in their late twenties and thirties determine what decisions they will need to make to get to their **End-of-Business-Life Paragraphs** and achieve their **Business Life Goals**. It is also a very revealing activity for professionals in their midforties to fifties, as it helps them discover if they have enough time left to achieve their **End-of-Business-Life Paragraph**. Many come to the realization that they do not have enough time left in their business life to become a senator, a doctor, or an attorney, and they must adjust their goals accordingly.

In yet another example, one mentee's **End-of-Business-Life Paragraph** had her being part of an international venture group for a specific type of service. As she worked backward, it was obvious to her that the position that she held and the company she was working for at the time would not be able to give her the background and skills she needed to advance to the next segment. So, she had to make a lateral move to another position, which enabled her to begin acquiring the necessary skills. She accepted a special assignment that enabled her to develop an understanding of the professional-services industry. She then left to join a startup company so as to continue along her journey toward her **End-of-Business-Life Paragraph**.

For leaders who follow this step-by-step process, the person working for you should have written their **End-of-Business-Life Paragraph** and defined the position that will enable it to happen. They should have completed their homework by researching and studying the lives and career paths of individuals who have held or currently hold their position of interest. They should have determined their educational path, the types of experiences they gained along the way, and the varieties of skills they developed.

By creating a composite of that end position, your subordinates now have an idea of the steps they will have to take—including the skills they will have to acquire, the relationships they will need to develop, and the educational experience required—in order to attain that position by the end of their business life. They may find that they need to accept positions that are completely different from those that they are currently engaged in order to obtain the skills that they will need for a future position in their life-planning segments.

This is an amazing retention tool available to any leader in any industry. When individuals realize that the work that they are doing is directly related to one of their **Business-Life Segments**, they will never leave that job, that assignment, and that organization. That is the most powerful link a leader can have with a direct or indirect report.

To illustrate what a **Business Life Plan** looks like, the following is a chart of an individual whose **End-of-**

Business-Life Paragraph had her working in a Fortune 50 company as its CIO, making presentations on the accomplishments of her organization. Looking at the skills and backgrounds of CIOs in Fortune 50 firms, she was able to understand what skills were required, and put those skills into three-year **Business Life Segments**.

Business-Life Planning Chart

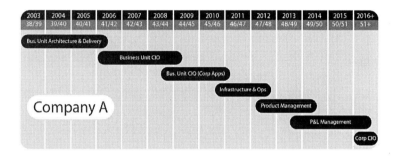

Encourage your subordinates to use this template to develop their own **Business-Life Planning Charts**. Modify the years reflected on the chart and the age range to suit the individual's station age and end-of-business-life goal.

While there is terrific power in understanding the skills, relationships, and experiences required to meet the **Business Life Goal**, there is an additional and very important element, and that is linking the **Business Life Plan** to an individual's **Personal Life Plan**. While this may seem an extension of the leader-subordinate relationship into the personal life realm, I have found that subordinates who allow the extension of that business-life planning to weave in personal-life planning draw even greater benefit from the process and gain an even greater sense of life security.

In Chapter Seven, we'll combine the **Business-Life Planning Chart** with the **Personal-Life Planning Chart** to show you how critical it is that your direct and indirect reports take their personal-life goals into account when planning their business life.

Chapter 6

Linking to Life Events

There is no question that real life for anyone is a blending of business and personal life. To not take this into account is making the mistake that the individual's **Business Life Goal** will be sabotaged by the activities that will rise and take center stage in their personal life. In creating a **Business Life Plan**, an individual must also look at his or her three-year segments in terms of what activities they will want to accomplish in their personal life.

Do they want to get an MBA or PhD? If they're not married, when do they believe they may want to get married? If they want to have children, when would they like that to happen? How many children do they want to have? And if they have children, when will they enter high school and college?

Each of these personal events also needs to be plotted in three-year segments so that the people in the organization will be able to map the skills, education, and experience he or she will need to obtain in harmony with the life experiences they desire to have—in essence, to parallel their **Business Life Goal** with their **Personal Life Goals**. There is power in linking a person's life activities with their business activities.

In addition to their personal three-year segments, there is the reality of an individual's personal finances and how those play out over the course of their business and personal life. It's important to understand when critical finances may be needed to fund an MBA, buy a home, finance the children's college education, or to buy a boat or even a second home. A personal life is as much a necessity to people as a business life.

In my years of experience in engaging with employees in this process, I have found that the ability to link their **Business Life Goals** with their **Personal Life Goals**—and financial goals—is a very powerful element in understanding how to retain people in your organization. If a person is at a point in their personal life where they need to accumulate a lot of income because their children are entering college, then they are going to make decisions that will enable them to generate as much income as possible.

Having that knowledge as a leader will help you recognize when somebody is potentially going to leave your organization for a much higher-paying job, even though it may not make sense in terms of their carefully thought-out **Business Life Plan**. So, the merging of those two plans helps the subordinate make rational business-life decisions.

I do understand that entering into an employee's personal life, especially around their financial situation and goals, may be an extension of the expected leader-subordinate relationship, and therefore has to be acknowledged and agreed to by the subordinate before the leader extends him or herself in the personal life of their direct or indirect reports.

To the extent that you as a leader can get that agreement, you will find it an extremely powerful tool. Yet you still need to maintain the degree of separation and privacy that's required in any business relationship. While linking into the personal and financial goals gives more power to the retention capabilities of a leader, if it's unable to be accomplished, the leader still has a solid connection to the **Business Life Goal** and **Business Life Segments** of the subordinate.

In my experience, I have found that employees are more than willing to share their personal goals and financial position with a leader on a purely voluntary, nonrequired basis. So, I encourage the leader to explore that dialogue with the individual to see if that connection can be made. Regardless of whether the personal-life information is shared with the supervisor, having an individual go through the process of creating a **Personal Life Plan** will make their **Business Life Plan** more realistic and meaningful. It's less important for you to see their **Personal Life Plan** than it is for the individual to actually produce one.

Going back to the example used in Chapter Five, the woman whose **Business Life Goal** was to be a CIO of a Fortune 50 company was willing to share her **Personal**

Life Goals and have us both view how her two planning charts intersected. Looking at the skills and backgrounds of CIOs in Fortune 50 firms, she was able to understand what skills were required and put those skills into three-year **Business Life Segments**.

Business Life Planning Chart

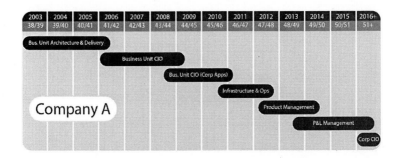

Once she charted out her **Business Life Plan** in three-year segments, she next needed to chart out her **Personal Life Plan**. As you can see from the chart below, she needed to get her MBA. She was also planning on having two children and to have them four years apart. Because of the leave that she would have to take for having the first child, she believed that she could, in fact, work on her MBA when she was home with the child.

Oftentimes, people will become more flexible in the types of positions they can hold once their children are of college age or have moved out on their own, so the attainment of skills or taking overseas assignments is more likely. We can see this reflected in her **Personal Life Plan**:

Personal Life Planning Chart

2003	2004	2005	2006	2007	2008	2009	2010	2011	2012	2013	2014	2015	2016+
38/39	39/40	40/41	41/42	42/43	43/44	44/45	45/46	46/47	47/48	48/49	49/50	50/51	51+

MBA

Marriage · Child · Child

Buy Lake House

Personal

It is vitally important for the employee to understand how the attainment of skills, knowledge, relationships, and experience interacts with their personal life. Having it linked and woven into their business life will give immense power and credence to their **Business Life Goal**. The objective is for them to understand their personal life enough so that it actually supplements and supports the attainment of the **Business Life Goal** versus working against the goal or derailing it completely.

The Six Steps to Business- and Personal-Life Planning

The process of building a **Business Life Plan** is a very worthwhile experience for leaders and their direct and indirect reports. It solidifies a bond between employees and a leader who, in my opinion, is stronger than any other because you, as the leader, are facilitating their attainment of their **Business Life Goals**. As mentioned earlier, I have found that this particular practice is the strongest retention tool that a leader can use.

To the extent that you can give your employees assignments that allow them to gain the skills and knowledge needed for their **Business Life Segment** or segments, they will stay with you as long as they are attaining those skills and experiences. In my experience, there is no greater way of solidifying that bond with an employee.

To begin the process of creating this indelible connection, I recommend the leader ask the employee to undertake the following six steps in developing their **Business Life Plan**:

1. Research the business-life paths of five individuals who currently hold your position of interest. Study their educational paths, job experiences, and skills developed.

2. Model your desired position by creating a composite of the life and career path of those five individuals.

3. Make a list of all the educational and skill requirements and map out how and when you will gain those life experiences up through to your desired point in your future.

4. Measure three-year segments by working back from that future point to where you are today. For example, if you are thirty-three years old and desire to retire at fifty-

four, you have seven actionable segments to obtain the education, experience, and skills needed to arrive at your future end point.

5. Parallel your three-year **Business Life Segments** with your **Personal Life Segments**, such as home ownership, marriage, family, the education of your children, etc.

6. Parallel your **Business Life Goals** and **Personal Life Goals** with your desired financial goals. To be effective, to be able to achieve what they want, there needs to be a certain amount of financial wealth accumulated at each segment. Your reports need to plot when they want to buy a new home, a second home, finance their children's college education, buy new cars, go on big vacations, and so on.

The **Business Life Goal** and **Business Life Segment** development processes are tools used by the leader to retain an individual and have them perform at their best. I would encourage the leader to be involved in trying to make sure that individuals under their leadership are on a path to reach their **Business Life Goals** and to be involved in giving them the skills, knowledge, and job experiences which will allow them to fulfill their **Business Life Segments** and achieve their goals.

Thus far, my book has presented my life as a transitional leader, having people assigned to me, and as a permanent leader, having individuals reporting directly to me. I have laid out four practices and processes for retaining individuals and inspiring them to perform at their best. What I have found is that this process has created a bridge into my post-retirement to the ultimate purpose of my being— my **Business Life Goal**.

I have, over the years, extended these processes to people who don't report to me and, in many instances, are complete strangers who have heard my speeches, read my book *Creating an Intentional Business Life*, or who have been referred to me by others whom I have helped. The next chapter will now define how I am living out my **Business Life Goal**.

Chapter 7

Living My Business Life Goal

Today, I no longer lead IT organizations or have people reporting to me. Rather, I am proceeding with my life as an investor in emerging businesses and as a board member. However, I am increasingly finding people drawing me into the role of mentor after having heard me speak or having read my work.

I have encountered people of all ages who find themselves at a crossroads in their lives and in their occupations, trying to decide whether they should take a new job or advanced position, go back to school for an MBA or PhD, or pursue their current professional track.

Many of them in their late thirties and early forties have been with their companies for ten years or longer and are doing very well. Now, for a variety of reasons, they have arrived at an impasse and are uncertain as to whether they should remain with their company, take a position in another company or industry, or pursue an advanced degree. And, as one would expect, these questions are amplified for people in their late forties and early fifties who suddenly realize that their choices are limited and the time left to execute those choices is diminishing.

Fran Dramis

There are many professionals surfing the waves of their skills and abilities who are uncertain as to where those waves are carrying them. They start early in their business lives, become fairly competent in their particular skill set, and are promoted based on their company's needs (not their own). Under the spell of their advancement—the increased responsibility, power, prestige, and income—they believe they are building a business life of value and have some semblance of control over their destiny.

Then, at some point, they arrive at a destination; they have ridden a wave of achievement that carried them to a certain place in their personal and professional lives, much in the same way a surfer rides a wave to a point on a shoreline. But they don't know exactly how they got there and aren't particularly content with where they landed. Though very competent and highly skilled, they never thought about where their career was carrying them. When asked to reflect back on their accomplishments, many of them cannot piece together how they arrived at their destination. Theirs was not an intentional **Business Life Plan**; they simply let their wave transport them. They cannot ascertain the significance or value of their professional journey, nor what it truly meant to their lives.

Upon reflection, they come to yet another realization that they never stopped to consider: the impact of the sacrifices they made along the way on their family and friends, or the ways in which they surrendered their own lives. They rode their waves for a decade or longer, passing opportunities along the shoreline that they could have explored at different points in their business life. Now, in the midst of or near the end of their working life, uneasiness wells up within them. They lament for not having taken another wave, for not having done something for themselves, for not having lived an intentional life.

When I first came to this realization, I was in my late thirties and was hearing it from people who were older than I was. It caused me to reflect and decide that, in fact, I was also a surfer. I was very good at what I was doing, and it just kept driving me forward. I finally asked the question, What if you could develop a **Business Life Plan** that, at the end of your working life, would have you feel like you controlled where you were going? How would I act if I knew what the end would look like and would be able to guarantee that the intervening time was worth my while?

With that in mind, I thought about my own business life and the things I had done so far. I'd always been driven to be a CEO of a company. I believed that the CEO position was like a brass ring. It was the highest position within a company, and so you ought to strive for that if you're going to be in business at all. I achieved a CEO position in my early forties, only to find out that there was something missing. It wasn't as fulfilling as I thought it was going to be. And as I started to reflect more on my life,

I realized that I had to figure out what I wanted to do with the remaining time I had in my business life.

I finally decided that what I really wanted to do was touch people's lives. In order to do that, I had to be able to influence their thought processes. I was not going to be able to accomplish that as a preacher or as a scholar. So, I knew that I was going to have to become a successful businessperson so that people would listen to me and accept my advice and coaching.

My drive for success from that point on was built around achieving success and position so that people would allow me to help them and to hear my points of view. That end goal turned out to be an incredible driver that underscored my business success. That drive to succeed also served as the main ingredient in my ability to retain key people. Over the thirty-year span of time that I was in business, I had over five hundred direct and indirect reports and had only lost one person whom I didn't want to lose.

I have discovered, especially during the last decade of my business life, that the **Business Life Plan** was in fact the real secret to retention. It allowed me to be enrolled in people's lives. It also allowed me to determine the types of positions along the way that would help me learn how to positively influence people. Keeping the end in mind, I formulated a mentoring process that would enable me to fulfill my dream of touching people's lives.

All of the previous chapters are really related to retaining people in positions. Almost by accident, I have found that the fulfillment of my **Business Life Goal** was to work with people who don't report to me outside of the business environment to help them attain their business life goal.

Over the course of my business life, as I have gone through the process of developing goals, plans, and segments with my direct and indirect reports, I had plenty of time to think about what I wanted to have as my **Business Life Goal**— to touch people's lives. And I was able to do that through the positional authority of being the top executive of various companies.

Yet today, no longer having that authority that comes with title, I wondered what I would do to realize my **Business Life Goal** in my post-retirement years. I discovered that in writing the book *Creating an Intentional Business Life*, I actually facilitated my goal by mentoring people who don't report to me or don't even have an association with me, people who were drawn to me by actually having read the book. I discovered that many individuals in a variety of professions and at different stages of their lives wanted to understand more about how I can help them. The concept was that unique and valuable to them.

After retiring from technology leadership positions, I was sought out by individuals who had either read my book or knew of my mentoring to be a life mentor for them. I have been extremely complimented by the trust that people have placed in me to help them attain their **Business Life Goal**.

I was recently mentoring a forty-year-old man who found himself faced with a decision: his firm was moving his organization overseas. He has three children, and did not want to make that move. Suddenly, he was faced with the question "what do I do now?" We sat down and walked through the creation of his **End-of-Business-Life Paragraph**, and that paragraph had certain attributes to it.

Those attributes led us to discover that he would like to have an end position of leading a technical-development group in the area of the intelligent power grid. It would be something that he would enjoy doing and feel worthwhile doing (contributing to society). At the same time, work in this particular industry would require him to stay within the United States, and also stay within this geographic region.

It was from that **End-of-Business-Life Paragraph** that we were able to then partition his life. He had seven segments left in his **Business Life Plan**. Knowing that, he was able to look at a possible array of positions that he could choose. The first one that came to mind was a special group that was a joint venture of his current company discovering how their technology would fit into the intelligent-power-grid industry. This was, of course, one of the skills required in his path to get to where he wanted to go. He accepted that position and sent me an amazing note that said, "I will never surf again. I will be more intentional in what I do from here on out."

Another is a person who just turned forty, has a brilliant mind, and is currently working as a pharmaceutical sales representative and has aspirations far beyond that. She feels unfulfilled in her current business and came to me asking for help. As a result of her writing her **End-of-Business-Life Paragraph**, she articulated wanting to make a presentation to the Supreme Court.

Obviously, the path between her age of forty and that end point—requiring obtaining her law degree—is going to be interesting. Getting a law practice is now on her path, in addition to taking the LSATs and applying to law school. She's obtaining money to get the most income she can, and is committed to passing her LSATs and going on to law school.

How Short Life Is

In another example, a middle-school athletic director whom I mentored decided that he wanted to be an athletic director for a top university. I gave him an assignment to profile the career paths of five athletic directors from various divisions of the Big 10, SEC, ACC, and other collegiate programs.

When he visited the university websites for their biographies or interviewed them, he discovered how they began their professional lives, what schools they attended, and what degrees they received. Did they work at their alma mater? When, over the course of their professions, did they make the transition to athletic director? Were they assistant athletic directors first? Who were their closest mentors and other professional relationships in their networks? Do the universities post professional and educational requirements for their athletic directors?

After doing all the background research and making a composite of the person who holds the athletic-director position, my mentee then had to divide his acquisition of the required skills and experiences into three-year segments leading up to his end position.

He was thirty-five and desired to be an athletic director by the time he was fifty-six years of age, so he had twenty-one years (or seven three-year actionable segments) to achieve his goal. The question then was, could he accomplish those life experiences in twenty-one years? It's quite revealing for everyone who starts to partition their skill acquisitions on this designated path of how short life is and how they need to "get on with" being more intentional in what they do in their business life. This is the most important benefit, I believe, to creating a **Business Life Plan**.

Being a personal mentor to individuals has truly enabled me to realize my **Business Life Goal**. In my **End-of-Business-Life Paragraph**, I'm sitting across the table from someone, helping them with their **Business Life Plan**, then intervening in their **Business Life Segments** to ensure that they are on track to completing their segments and attaining their goal. That process fulfills my lifelong ambition of being meaningful in people's lives by helping them determine a much more meaningful and fulfilling path for themselves in the many years that will comprise their business life.

I encourage the reader of this book to not only use the techniques as a retention tool, but to consider the value that you have as a leader in mentoring people anywhere and at any time. If you're like me, you'll find that your business success pales in comparison to the feeling that you have when someone acknowledges your significance in his or her life by sending you a text that says, "It's really because of your mentoring that I was able to achieve what I have in my business life."

Endnotes

[1] "A 21st Century Update on Employee Tenure," Employee Benefit Research Institute, March 2001, vol. 22, no. 3, https://www.ebri.org/pdf/notespdf/0301notes.pdf.

[2] Bureau of Labor and Statistics, "Employee Tenure Summary," January 2016, http://www.bls.gov/news.release/tenure.nr0.htm.

[3] "2016 State of the CIO Survey," *CIO* magazine, January 2016, http://core0.staticworld.net/assets/2016/01/14/2016-state-of-the-cio-executive-summary.pdf.

[4] "Automobiles," History.com, http://www.history.com/topics/automobiles.

[5] Ibid.

[6] Alfred P. Sloan, "Critical Evaluations in Business and Management," John C. Wood (New York: Rutledge, December, 2003), 197.

[7] Ibid.

[8] "W. Edwards Deming, Expert on Business Management, Dies at 93," *New York Times*, December 21, 1993, http://www.nytimes.com/1993/12/21/obituaries/w-edwards-deming-expert-on-business-management-dies-at-93.html?pagewanted=all.

[9] Doug McInnis, "W. Edwards Deming of Powell, Wyo.: The Man Who Helped Shape the World,"

http://www.wyohistory.org/encyclopedia/w-edwards-deming.

[10] Ibid.

[11] "Downsizing and Rightsizing," Reference for Business, http://www.referenceforbusiness.com/management/De-Ele/Downsizing-and-Rightsizing.html.

[12] Ibid.

[13] "System/360 Announcement," IBM Archives, https://www-03.ibm.com/ibm/history/exhibits/mainframe/mainframe_PR360.html.

[14] Ibid.

[15] "Downsizing," *The Economist*, July 28, 2008, http://www.economist.com/node/11773794.

[16] "MCI: The End of a Telecom Icon," February 15, 2005, http://www.cnet.com/news/mci-the-end-of-a-telecom-icon/.

[17] Ibid.

[18] "The Four Industries with the Worst Retention Rates," TINYpulse, May 23, 2016, https://www.tinypulse.com/blog/industries-with-the-worst-retention-rates.

[19] "Tech Companies Have Highest Turnover Rate," http://www.techrepublic.com/blog/career-management/tech-companies-have-highest-turnover-rate/.

[20] Frank Buytendijk, "Corporate Performance Management Helps Build High-Performance Organizations," August 2005.

[21] Jim Collins and Jerry Porras, *Built to Last: Successful Habits of Visionary Companies* (1994), 251.

[22] Patrick Lencioni, "Make Your Values Mean Something," *Harvard Business Review* (2002).

[23] "Enron's Vision (and Values) Thing," *New York Times*, January 19, 2002, http://www.nytimes.com/2002/01/19/opinion/enron-s-vision-and-values-thing.html.

About the Author

Fran Dramis is recognized as one of the nation's top strategic executives for his leadership and innovativeness. He is the CEO of F. Dramis LLC, an author, investor, and a member of multiple public and private boards. Fran is a frequent speaker at leadership forums and is a business life mentor, helping individuals chart a career path to a fulfilling business and personal life.